THE AUSTRALIA SURVIVAL GUIDE

PUFFIN BOOKS

UK | USA | Canada | Ireland | Australia
India | New Zealand | South Africa | China

 Penguin
Random House
Australia

Penguin Random House Australia is part of the Penguin Random House group of companies
whose addresses can be found at global.penguinrandomhouse.com.

First published by Puffin Books, an imprint of Penguin Random House Australia Pty Ltd, in 2019

Cover design by Bruno Herfst & Tony Palmer © Penguin Random House Australia Pty Ltd
Internal design, illustration and typesetting by Astred Hicks, Design Cherry
Cover images by: animal illustrations LittleAirplane/Shutterstock.com; warning sign JONGSUK/
Shutterstock.com; paper background Vitaly Korovin/Shutterstock.com; splatter/Shutterstock.com

Printed and bound in China

 A catalogue record for this
book is available from the
National Library of Australia

ISBN 978 01 43 79657 2 (Hardback)

Penguin Random House Australia uses papers that are natural, renewable and recyclable products
and made from wood grown in sustainable forests. The logging and manufacturing processes are
expected to conform to the environmental regulations of the country of origin.

penguin.com.au

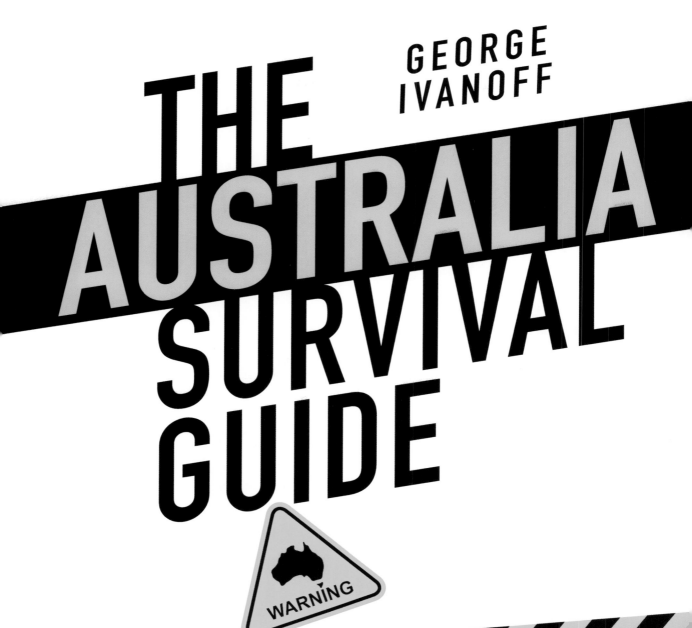

GEORGE
IVANOFF

THE AUSTRALIA SURVIVAL GUIDE

WARNING

AUSTRALIA IS TRYING TO **KILL** YOU — THIS BOOK WILL SAVE YOUR LIFE!

PUFFIN BOOKS

For Michael, Karen and Alyssa. For Margaret, Andreas, Tori and Nicholas. For Emily, Malcolm, Sarah and Zoe.
Thanks for sharing Australia with us . . . and for helping us survive.

CONTENTS

Introduction
9

ON LAND
12

Slithering Death
15

Creepy Crawly Death
25

Tiny Flying Vampiric Death
35

Tiny Not-Quite Death
41

Cute but ~~Deadly~~ Dangerous
43

Totally Fake Death Part 1
49

IN THE WATER
52

**Swimming Death
Part 1**

**Swimming Death
Part 2**

Tentacled Death

**Wibbly-Wobbly
Jelly Death**

**Totally Fake
Death Part 2**

THE ENVIRONMENT
86

Hot Thirsty Death
89

Leafy Death
101

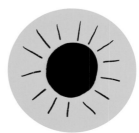

Death from Above
111

Sandy Drowning Death
117

The Four Elements of Death
123

Not Death (Bush Tucker and Bush Medicine)
133

EVERYTHING ELSE
(NOT ALL OF IT INVOLVING DEATH)
140

Civilisation
143

Big Things
151

Random Stuff
155

INTRODUCTION

HELP!

I'm in MORTAL DANGER!

For real!

I'm used to everything trying to kill me in video games. But this is no game. This is REALITY! SCARY REALITY!

For 13 years, I've lived a nice, safe life in the suburbs. The worst things I had to worry about were homework and choosing which game to play next.

But now my parents have put my life in JEOPARDY!

They're dragging me all across Australia, through deserts and bushlands, into the path of venomous snakes, deadly spiders, vicious crocs, hungry sharks, maybe even cyclones and bushfires . . .

The list goes on and on.

Why?

They're calling this a *holiday*. They reckon it's gonna be fun. They keep telling me I'll enjoy the adventure.

But seriously . . . they're NUTS!

I've done the research. I've been to the library . . . I've browsed online . . . I've read the newspapers . . . I know just how DANGEROUS Australia really is. This 'holiday' is putting my life in PERIL! And I can't hide behind a game avatar.

So, to make sure I do not die in vain . . .

To save the lives of other kids in the future . . .

I am going to document how AUSTRALIA IS TRYING TO KILL YOU and how you might be able to SURVIVE! Preparation and information are the keys. I am going to gather up all the info I can and put it into this guide, giving you the benefit of my research and wisdom. Helping you to prepare for the HORRORS that may be waiting for you.

Wish me luck. I'm gonna need it!

DEAD-O-METER

Most things in Australia can KILL YOU! (Okay . . . not *most* . . . but there are LOTS!) But how badly can they kill you? I've devised a scale for measuring just how dead you'll be. Presenting the Dead-O-Meter . . .

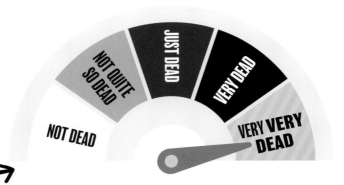

BANDAID

This was the bandaid used to fix my worst ever injury – a blister on my finger from 42 hours, 19 minutes and 7 seconds of school holiday binge gaming (it could have been longer if not for my parents launching an intervention). But now I'm being threatened by vicious bites, deadly stings, dehydration, humungous hailstones and MANY, MANY, MANY other things and creatures far more LETHAL than a gaming blister! I'm gonna need a bigger bandaid.

GLOSSARY

When researching all this dangerous stuff about Australia, I kept hitting words and terms that I didn't understand. I'd have to stop reading and go look 'em up in dictionaries and encyclopedias. Annoying! To make things easier for you, I've put together a glossary at the end of this guide, to explain all those things. So, whenever there's a circled word or term in this guide, you can go look at the glossary on page 165 for an explanation. And you never have to leave the comfort of this book. Pretty cool, huh?

AVATAR

This is me! Well, it's game me. My online gaming avatar. I reckon I'm gonna need all my game-playing survival skills to get me through this holiday. The only problem is – if you die in real life, you can't re-spawn!

SECTION ONE

ON LAND

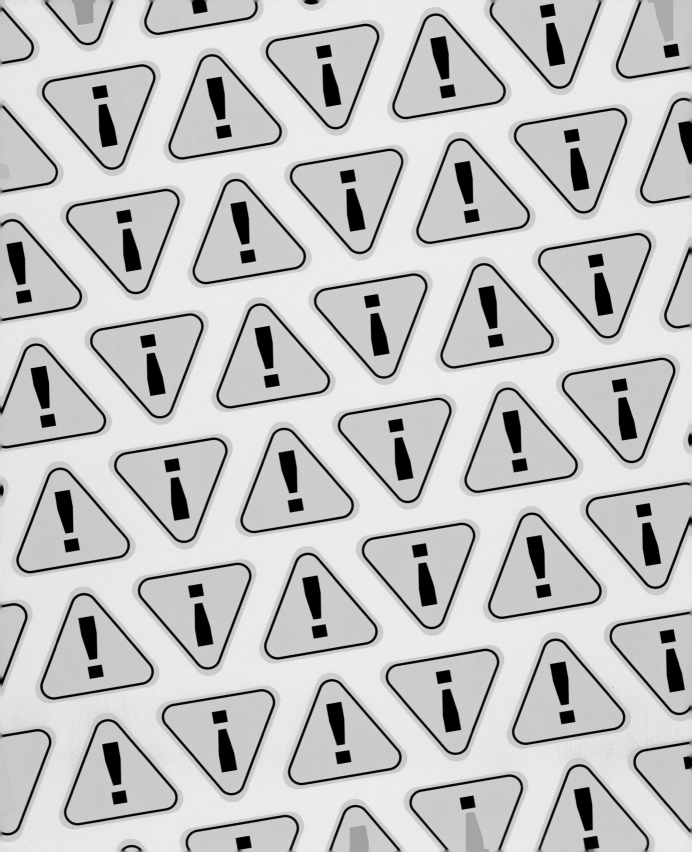

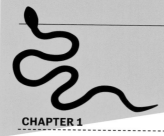

CHAPTER 1

SLITHERING DEATH

Snakes are cold-blooded reptiles. There are over 2900 species worldwide and over 100 of them are in Australia. They slither around and sneak up on you. They eat animals by swallowing them WHOLE! They don't have eyelids, which is kinda creepy. But they do have FANGS! And they want to kill you! HEEEEEEEELP!

Okay . . . so I've found out that not all of them want to kill you. But loads of Australian snakes are deadly – 39 of them. Plus there are lots more that are dangerous, even if they won't kill you.

AUSTRALIA'S TOP 10 DEADLIEST SNAKES

1. Eastern brown snake
2. Western brown snake
3. Tiger snake
4. Inland taipan
5. Coastal taipan
6. Mulga snake
7. Lowlands copperhead
8. Small-eyed snake
9. Common death adder
10. Red-bellied black snake

Hey . . . I noticed that different websites and books list these snakes in different orders. It's like people can't agree on which ones are more likely to kill you. Crikey! But at least it's always the same ten snakes, and the Eastern brown snake is usually in the number one spot.

Okay, so a snake bite isn't an automatic DEATH SENTENCE. That's good to know.

Envenoming

According to the World Health Organisation an estimated 5.4 million people worldwide are bitten by snakes each year, but only up to 2.7 million of those bites result in envenoming.

Envenoming occurs when the snake's venom enters the bloodstream. But not all snakes are venomous and not all cases of snakebite from a venomous snake result in venom entering the victim. If envenoming does occur, antivenom may need to be administered to stop or reverse the effects of the venom.

FACT FILE

Common name

EASTERN BROWN SNAKE

Also known as

Common brown snake

Scientific name

Pseudonaja textilis

Size

Up to 2.5 metres, but usually about 1.5 metres

Habitat

Wide-ranging, from forests to deserts, but not in rainforests

Location

Eastern half of mainland Australia

Prey

Lizards, birds, frogs and small mammals

Effects of venom

Progressive paralysis; stops blood from clotting

Other stuff you need to know

- Eastern brown snakes are fast, bad tempered and aggressive. They may attack if disturbed, so stay away from them.

- They are responsible for the most snakebites in Australia and the highest number of deaths.

- Although it's called a 'brown snake', the colour of individual snakes can vary from tan to brown to black.

- When threatened, they will rear up into an 'S' shape and hiss loudly with an open mouth.

- Their venom is the second-most toxic of any land snake in the world.

- They can be found around farms where there are lots of rats and mice.

FACT FILE

Common name

WESTERN BROWN SNAKE

Also known as

Gwardar

Scientific name

Pseudonaja aspidorhyncha, Pseudonaja mengdeni, Pseudonaja nuchalis

Size

Up to 1.5 metres

Habitat

Arid and semi-arid areas such as deserts, grasslands, shrublands and forests

Location

Most of Australia

Prey

Small reptiles such as skinks and other snakes, birds, small mammals such as rats

Effects of venom

Headaches, nausea, abdominal pain, stops blood from clotting and can cause kidney damage

Other stuff you need to know

- The common name of western brown snake actually covers three species of snakes.

- Western brown snakes are fast and nervous. If disturbed, they will usually slither away as quickly as they can. But if cornered, they will attack.

- Their venom is not as strong as that of the eastern brown snake, but their bite delivers three times the amount.

- The western brown's bite is often painless and can be hard to see because of their small fangs. *Very sneaky.*

- They can be either golden brown or orange, with a pale or dark head.

Common name

TIGER SNAKE

Also known as

Mainland tiger snake

Scientific name

Notechis scutatus

Size

Up to 2 metres, but usually about 0.9 metres

Habitat

Near water or areas that receive a lot of rain

Location

Southern coastal areas of Australia, from Western Australia to New South Wales; small coastal areas of southern Queensland; and Tasmania

Prey

Mostly frogs, but also mammals, lizards, birds and smaller snakes

Effects of venom

Pain in feet and neck, tingling, numbness, sweating, trouble breathing, paralysis and damages the blood and muscles

Other stuff you need to know

- Tiger snakes come in a variety of colours, including dark blue, brown, grey and black. Usually, but not always, they are patterned with yellow stripes, which is why they're called tiger snakes.

- Even though they are sometimes called 'mainland' tiger snakes they also live in Tasmania.

- They are aggressive and are responsible for the second-highest number of snakebites in Australia.

FACT FILE

Common name

INLAND TAIPAN

Also known as

Fierce snake, small-scaled snake, lignum snake

Scientific name

Oxyuranus microlepidotus

Size

Up to 2.5 metres, usually about 1.5 metres

Habitat

Dry, rocky plains

Location

South-western Queensland and north-eastern South Australia

Prey

Small to medium mammals, mostly rats

Effects of venom

Headache, nausea, vomiting, abdominal pain and paralysis

Other stuff you need to know

- Inland taipans are the most venomous snakes on Earth. If bitten, seek medical attention immediately.

- Despite their nickname – fierce snakes – they are actually quite shy and not at all fierce. It's rare for these snakes to bite humans.

- They are pale to dark brown in colour.

OMG! Just run away now!

FACT FILE

FACT FILE

Common name
COASTAL TAIPAN

Also known as
Eastern taipan

Scientific name
Oxyuranus scutellatus

Size
Up to 2.8 metres, usually about 2 metres

Habitat
Wide variety of coastal areas, from cane fields to woodlands

Location
Northern and eastern coasts of Australia

Prey
Mostly small- to medium-sized mammals

Effects of venom
Headaches, nausea, convulsions, paralysis, internal bleeding and kidney damage

Other stuff you need to know
- Coastal taipans have the longest fangs of any Australian snake. Their fangs are about 12 millimetres.
- They are aggressive if threatened.
- If you get a large dose of venom, death can occur in only 30 minutes.

That's hardly enough time to write out your will.

- They vary in colour from brown and black to coppery red and olive.

FACT FILE

Common name
MULGA SNAKE

Also known as
King brown snake

Scientific name
Pseudechis australis

Size
Up to 2.7 metres

Habitat
Widespread, from tropical areas to sandy deserts

Location
In every state except Victoria and Tasmania

Prey
Frogs, reptiles, birds, mammals, and reptile and bird eggs

Effects of venom
Swelling, bruising and pain around the area of the bite, muscle damage, kidney damage and stops blood from clotting

Other stuff you need to know
- Mulga snakes come in various shades of brown and sometimes black.
- When they bite, they often hang on or bite multiple times as if they are chewing.
- Even though they're known as 'king brown snakes', they are actually members of the black snake family. So bites need to be treated with black snake antivenom, not brown snake antivenom.

Huh? This is confusing. Don't these snakes know which family they belong to?

Common name

COPPERHEAD

(There are three species: pygmy, highlands, lowlands.)

Scientific name

Austrelaps labialis, Austrelaps ramsayi, Austrelaps superbus

Size

Between 84 centimetres and 1.7 metres, depending on the species

Habitat

Cooler areas near water

Location

South-eastern Australia, in South Australia, Victoria, New South Wales, Tasmania and the islands of Bass Strait

Prey

Frogs, tadpoles, small lizards and mice

Effects of venom

Damages the nerves, blood cells and muscles

Other stuff you need to know

- Lowlands copperheads can be black, grey or brown in colour, with a copper-coloured head.
- They are shy and will usually try to stay away from people.
- If cornered, they will usually hiss and thrash about, but rarely bite.
- They are able to live in cooler places than most other snakes.

FACT FILE

Common name

SMALL-EYED SNAKE

Also known as

Eastern small-eyed snake

Scientific name

Cryptophis nigrescens

Size

Up to 1.2 metres, usually about 0.5 metres

Habitat

High-moisture habitats, including rainforests, woodlands and rocky areas

Location

Across eastern Australia, from Queensland to Victoria

Prey

Lizard eggs and small reptiles, mostly skinks

Effects of venom

Damages muscle tissue

Other stuff you need to know

- The eyes of small-eyed snakes are small and darkly coloured.
- They are secretive and unlikely to be out in the open during the day so rarely come into contact with humans.
- These snakes are sometimes cannibalistic, eating smaller members of their own species.

Idea for a horror film – *Attack of the Small-eyed Cannibal Snakes.* Hollywood, here I come!

FACT FILE

FACT FILE

Common name

COMMON DEATH ADDER

Also known as

Coastal death adder or southern death adder

Scientific name

Acanthophis antarcticus

Size

Up to 1 metre, usually 0.5–0.6 metres

Habitat

Forests and grasslands

Location

New South Wales and Queensland, as well as the southern areas of Western Australia and South Australia

Prey

Frogs, lizards and birds

Effects of venom

Drooping eyelids, nausea, difficulty speaking, difficulty breathing and paralysis

Other stuff you need to know

- Common death adders have triangular-shaped heads; short, thick bodies and thin tails.
- Their colours vary greatly, from grey to red.
- They do not hunt their prey. They stay in one spot, hiding under leaves, sand or gravel, and wait for prey to come to them.
- They attack with lightning speed.
- When threatened they will usually stay still and try to blend in with their surroundings.

FACT FILE

Common name

RED-BELLIED BLACK SNAKE

Also known as

Common black snake

Scientific name

Pseudechis porphyriacus

Size

Up to 2 metres, usually 1–1.2 metres

Habitat

Forests and grasslands near water

Location

East coast of Queensland, New South Wales and Victoria, and in small parts of south-eastern South Australia

Prey

Fish, tadpoles, frogs, lizards, snakes and mammals

Effects of venom

Swelling around bite, blood-clotting, nausea, headaches, abdominal pain, diarrhoea, sweating, muscle pain and weakness

Other stuff you need to know

- Red-bellied black snakes are mostly black, with red/orange sides and belly.

  > Duh! That's why they're called red-bellied black snakes.

- They hunt on both land and in water and often go into water with just their heads above the surface. And they can stay under water for over 20 minutes.
- A bite from a red-bellied black is rarely life-threatening to a human.

Survival
Flying Doctors Save Snake-bitten Teen

February 2009

It was the Royal Flying Doctor Service (RFDS) to the rescue, when teenager Rhianna Harvie was bitten by a mulga snake while sleeping in her Blinman home. Thanks to first-aid advice provided over the phone by an RFDS doctor and then a night flight to Royal Adelaide Hospital, Rhianna survived the snake encounter.

Blinman is a small town in South Australia's Flinders Rangers, about 500 kilometres from Adelaide. Returning to her hometown for the weekend, after enrolling in an Animal Science degree at Adelaide University, Rhianna encountered an uninvited visitor.

It had been a hot evening, Rhianna decided to sleep on a mattress in the lounge room, where a new air conditioner had been installed. At about 11 pm she was woken by a sudden, sharp pain in her left upper thigh. It turns out that a two-metre long mulga snake had decided to share her mattress and had bitten her twice.

Rhianna's stepfather quickly tied a dressing gown cord around the top of her thigh as a tourniquet, above the bite, to stop the spread of venom and then contacted the RFDS. A RFDS doctor talked him through the necessary first aid. He needed to slow the flow of blood in the leg by putting a compression bandage around the whole leg, rather than just using a tourniquet. Not having a compression bandage, he improvised by tightly wrapping the entire leg in a sheet. Then he had to get Rhianna to the designated spot where they would meet the RFDS plane, which had been dispatched from the base at Port Augusta.

Rhianna was driven from Blinman, through Parachilna Gorge, to the Outback Highway, where she was met by an ambulance. The ambulance then raced her to the closest airstrip in the town of Hawker. From there she was flown to Adelaide and treated at the Royal Adelaide Hospital, where she received the required antivenom.

Wow! Imagine being bitten by a snake so far from a hospital, that you needed the RFDS to come and get you. The RFDS are amazing! Check out this website to see all the fab work they do: flyingdoctor.org.au

FUN SNAKE FACTS

* Snakes are reptiles.

* Snakes do not have eyelids. Instead they have a transparent layer over each eye, called a spectacle.

* Snakes do not have tear ducts.

> Boo-hoo! They can't cry!

* Snakes do not have ears. They have special bones inside their heads that pick up sound vibrations. But they can't pick up high-pitched sounds like birdsong.

* Snakes are cold-blooded.

* Snakes are covered in scales, which are made of keratin (the same substance that our hair, fingernails and toenails are made of).

* Snakes shed their skin as they grow.

* Twenty of the world's most venomous snakes live in Australia.

* Snakes swallow their food whole rather than chewing.

* Some snakes lay eggs, but others give birth to live babies.

FIRST AID

DO:

✓ Keep the patient calm and as still as possible.

✓ Call an ambulance.

✓ Apply a pressure immobilisation bandage, if you have one (this will slow down the spread of the venom). This is a bandage used to wrap an entire limb tightly and also has a splint to stop it from moving. Start the bandage at the tip of the limb and work up.

DO NOT:

✗ DO NOT wash the bite area (any venom left on the skin could help identify the type of snake that caused the bite).

✗ DO NOT apply a tourniquet.

✗ DO NOT cut the wound.

✗ DO NOT try to suck out the venom.

> Fear not! (Well . . . maybe fear a little.) If you get bitten by a snake, you won't necessarily DIE! There is still HOPE! There is FIRST AID!

> I remember seeing a movie where some guy got bitten by a snake. His friend used a knife to cut open the wound, then he sucked out the venom. It was a bit YUCK! And the WRONG thing to do.

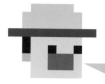

Mum and Dad reckon it's better not to need first aid. That is, DON'T GET BITTEN. So, if you're visiting an area that might have snakes, here's what you should do . . .

HOW TO AVOID BEING BITTEN

- Look where you are walking.
- Stay away from tall grass.
- Don't stick your hand or foot into crevasses and holes.
- Wear protective clothing (boots and long pants).
- If you see a snake, don't go near it. Slowly back away.

SNAKES AS PETS

I wouldn't want to have a snake as a pet, but it looks like some people do. Some pet stores specialise in snakes and other reptiles! And you may need to get a license to own certain types of reptiles.

There are several types of non-venomous pythons that make good pets: Children's python, Stimson's python, and the woma (black-headed python). I think I'd rather get a goldfish!

FACT FILE

Common name

CHILDREN'S PYTHON

Scientific name
Antaresia childreni

Size
Usually about 1 metre

Habitat
Dry forests, grasslands, coastal plains, dry riverbeds and rocky areas

Location
Northern and central Australia

Prey
Small lizards, small mammals and frogs

Other stuff you need to know
- Children's pythons are named after John George Children, the zoologist who first described this species in 1842.

- They are gentle and easy to handle, which is why they make good pets.
- These snakes are brown with dark markings. Their scales can have an iridescent blue sheen.
- They kill their prey by squeezing it to death. If keeping one as a pet, you need to feed it 1–2 mice a week.

But I thought they were called children's pythons because they ate children.

Never trust a snake . . . not even a Children's python. I reckon it's best to just STAY AWAY from all snakes. Just in case.

But if you really want to see one, go to a zoo or a reptile park. That way, they can't bite you. And you can appreciate how they come in an amazing range of colours and sizes. And how they have different head shapes. And how they move with such calm grace. Um . . . not that I like them. I DON'T! But . . . you know . . . they might be worth checking out.

Here's a pic of a coastal taipan that I snapped at the zoo . . . from behind a THICK glass window.

CHAPTER 2

CREEPY CRAWLY DEATH

Arachnophobia

noun
irrational fear of spiders.

There is nothing irrational about a fear of spiders!!!

SPIDER VENOM

Spiders only put a small amount of venom into their victims when they bite them. It's meant for small prey, so their venom is not as dangerous to human beings. Even though we have antivenom for funnel-web and redback bites, they aren't often used. Antivenom is only needed in severe cases. The people most at risk from spider bites are the very young, the elderly and people with cardiovascular disease.

This means problems with the heart and/or blood vessels.

I don't have arachnophobia, but I still think spiders are the creepiest things EVER! They're icky and . . . and . . . evil and . . . they can kill you (well, some of them), and . . . I don't like them. But I'm not arachnophobic! OKAY!

Calm down!

Australia does have some of the most venomous spiders in the world. (First snakes! Now spiders! I'm sensing a bit of a pattern here.) But because of modern medicine and the availability of antivenom, hardly anyone dies from a spider bite. Spiders are supposedly less deadly than snakes or sharks or bees. Hang on . . . bees? Some researchers reckon that more people die from allergic reactions to bee stings than from spider bites, because they go into anaphylactic shock. Wow!

AUSTRALIA'S TOP 5 DEADLIEST SPIDERS

There are LOTS of different funnel-web spiders. But the Sydney funnel-web is the WORST! So it gets a spot all of its own.

1. Sydney funnel-web
2. Other Australian funnel-webs
3. Redback spider
4. Mouse spider
5. Trapdoor spider

Honourable mention:
Huntsman – see Fact File to find out why.

FACT FILE

Common name

AUSTRALIAN FUNNEL-WEB SPIDER

Scientific name

Hexathelidae – this is their family name. There are three subfamilies: *Atracinae*, *Hexathelinae* and *Plesiothelinae*. Only the 35 types of funnel-web in the *Atracinae* subfamily are dangerous to humans

Size

14–55 millimetres body length (not including legs)

Habitat

Moist, cool, sheltered habitats

Location

Coastal eastern Australia and parts of South Australia

Web

Fine silk, used to line its burrow

Prey

Ground insects, snails and small skinks

Effects of venom

Pain at bite site, tingling around mouth, sweating, salivation, difficulty swallowing, difficulty breathing, abdominal pain, vomiting, muscle twitching, disorientation and unconsciousness (The severity of reactions can vary depending on the exact type of funnel-web and whether it is male or female)

Other stuff you need to know

- Antivenom has been available since 1981. No deaths have been recorded since the introduction of antivenom.

- Drops of venom are formed on the tips of the spider's fangs and are then pushed through the victim's skin when it bites. The venom isn't injected, so a funnel-web bite often doesn't come with venom.

- Once a funnel-web has used all its venom, it can take up to two weeks before it has another full dose.

- Funnel-web spiders live in silk-lined burrows in the ground and in rotting logs, surrounded by silk 'trip-lines'. There are also a few types that make their burrows in trees.

- At night, funnel-webs wait for their prey to pass by their burrows, then they pounce.

- Male spiders will go off in search of females during spring and summer. This is when bites most often happen.

- These spiders are large and shiny black to dark brown in colour.

- The venom of the male spider is more toxic than the female.

Scientific Names

The scientific names get a bit confusing. There are groupings within groupings, each getting more specific. Each spider is part of a species, which is part of a genus, which is part of a family, which is part of an order, which is part of a class. Some even have subfamilies between the genus and the main family. Wow . . . that's confusing. I can't keep track of it all. I'll just keep referring to them as TERRIFYING!

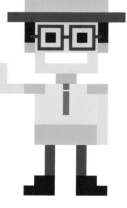

Common name

SYDNEY FUNNEL-WEB SPIDER

Scientific name

Atrax robustus

Size

20–30 millimetres body length

Habitat

Moist, cool, sheltered habitats

Location

Mostly in the Sydney area, but also in smaller numbers in the rest of coastal New South Wales as well as parts of regional Victoria and Queensland

Web

Fine silk used to line its burrow

Prey

Ground insects, snails and small skinks

Effects of venom

Pain at bite site, tingling around mouth, sweating, salivation, difficulty swallowing, trouble breathing, abdominal pain, vomiting, muscle twitching, disorientation and unconsciousness

Other stuff you need to know

- Sydney funnel-web spiders are the deadliest of the funnel-web spiders.
- If bitten, you can die in as little as 15 minutes.
- They are aggressive.
- They are shiny black to dark brown in colour.

FACT FILE

Common name

REDBACK SPIDER

Scientific name

Latrodectus Hasseltii (family: *Theridiidae*)

Size

Up to 12 millimetres

Habitat

Prefers dry places

Location

Australia-wide

Web

Tangled webs with a funnel-like area for the spider to hide in

Prey

Insects, snakes, lizards, mice

> Wow! They eat big for such little critters.

Effects of venom

Pain spreading out from bite site, sweating, nausea, headache and paralysis in severe cases

Other stuff you need to know

- Female redback spiders are black with a red stripe on their backs. But the smaller males are brown with red and white markings.
- Only the female spiders have a dangerous bite.
- Redback spiders can lay up to 1500 eggs in one season.
- No deaths have been recorded since the introduction of antivenom in 1956.
- They are not usually aggressive and only bite if disturbed.

FACT FILE

FACT FILE

Common name

MOUSE SPIDER

Scientific name

Actinopodidae (family)

Size

10–35 millimetres body length

Habitat

Forest and shrubland areas

Location

Mainland Australia

Web

Uses silk to line its burrow in the ground

Prey

Ground insects, other spiders, small lizards and frogs

Effects of venom

Similar to a funnel-web spider, but it is rare for a bite to envenom

Other stuff you need to know

- Mouse spiders are often mistaken for funnel-web spiders, but their legs are shorter.

  I don't care which one it is . . . I don't want it anywhere near me.

- Mouse spiders have shiny black, dark purple or dark blue bodies, some with red markings.

- Their venom is similar to the funnel-web spider, so funnel-web antivenom can be used to treat bites.

- They often dry-bite humans, saving their venom for actual prey.

  Oh, aren't they considerate? NOT!

- There are eight different types of mouse spider in Australia.

FACT FILE

Common name

TRAPDOOR SPIDER

Scientific name

The name 'trapdoor spider' covers a range of spiders in an order called *Mygalomorphae* (which includes mouse spiders and funnel-web spiders). While each different trapdoor spider has its own scientific name, there is no one scientific name for the group

Size

1.5–3 centimetres body length

Habitat

Drier areas

Location

Mainly eastern Australia

Web

Uses silk to line its burrow

Prey

Ground insects like grasshoppers and beetles, other spiders and sometimes moths

Effects of venom

Pain at bite site, swelling

Other stuff you need to know

- Trapdoor spiders live in burrows in the ground, often with a door made from soil, vegetation and silk. When prey comes near enough, the spider flips back the door and pounces with lightning speed.

- Their name is misleading because not all trapdoor spiders have doors on their burrows.

- Their bites are painful and can make you feel unwell, but they're not deadly to humans.

- Trapdoor spiders can live up to 20 years.

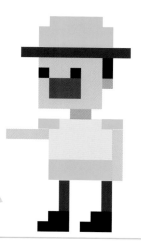

Spider Size
They all look bigger than their official size. That's because they're measured by body length. But what about the legs? Some spider have REALLY LONG legs. A Tasmanian cave spider has a body length of only 1.3–2 centimetres, but a leg span of up to 18 centimetres. 18 centimetres!!!!!! Aaaarggggggghhhhh!

Common name

HUNTSMAN

Scientific name
Sparassidae

Size
Length: up to 4.5 centimetres; leg span: up to 15 centimetres

Habitat
In the wild, they tend to live under bark and rocks, but they are commonly found indoors

Location
Australia-wide

Web
None

Prey
Insects

Effects of venom
Pain at bite site

Other stuff you need to know

- There are almost 100 different types of huntsman spiders worldwide of varying colours, including one that is bright green.

- Although they look hairy and scary, they are actually quite shy. If disturbed, they will usually run away rather than bite.

- They are fast and often scuttle out from behind things where they've been hiding – curtains, boxes, sun visors in cars – causing people to panic and have accidents. People have injured themselves falling off ladders and crashing vehicles because of scuttling huntsman spiders.

- Huntsman spiders live for about two years.

FACT FILE

This is why I hate them!!! The way they scuttle about is seriously CREEPY!

While some spiders are DANGEROUS or DEADLY, there are some that aren't as DANGEROUS as people think they are. Like the white-tailed spider. It's pretty small, but it's the biggest fake . . .

NOT QUITE SO DEAD — JUST DEAD — VERY DEAD — NOT DEAD — VERY VERY DEAD

BIGGEST FAKE

WHITE-TAILED SPIDER (*LAMPONIDAE*)

For years, these spiders have had a reputation for their dangerous necrotising bite. But this is a myth. Although some people have claimed to have rotting ulcers as the result of a white-tail spider bite, it has never been scientifically proven. Although a white-tail bite can hurt and cause redness and itchiness, it is not dangerous.

> This means the bite will cause a large chunk of your flesh to die and rot away. Eeeww! Gross!

> OMG! That's over 100 million years BEFORE the dinosaurs. These creatures are prehistoric!

FUN SPIDER FACTS

* There have been no officially confirmed spider bite deaths in Australia since 1979.

* There are over 34,000 species of spider in the world and about 10,000 of them are in Australia.

* We know from fossils that spiders first evolved more than 350 million years ago.

* Most spiders have eight eyes. But there are some that have only two. And some that have six.

Spider Invasion

May 2015

Spiders rained down over Goulburn in the early morning, covering the area with masses of webbing. Residents woke to a baby spider invasion!

This phenomenon, also called 'angel hair', is rare and requires special weather conditions. It only happens in May or August, during the spider-hatching season. Baby spiders float through the air on silk threads (this is called 'ballooning'), carried by the wind, sometimes for hundreds of kilometres, coming to land over fields and farms.

OMG! I am NEVER going to Goulburn!

FIRST AID

DO:

✓ Funnel-web and mouse spider bites need to be treated as quickly as possible. Use a pressure immobilisation bandage.

✓ Get the victim to keep as still as possible.

✓ Other spider bites do not need a bandage. That will just make the pain worse.

✓ Wash the wound. (The opposite of what you do with a snake bite.)

✓ Use a cold pack if the bite is painful.

✓ Get medical help as quickly as possible.

✓ Catch the spider so it can be identified.

DO NOT:

✗ DO NOT apply a tourniquet.

✗ DO NOT cut the wound.

✗ DO NOT try to suck out the venom.

✗ DO NOT let the victim eat or drink anything.

HOW TO CATCH A SPIDER:

- Put an empty jar over the spider.
- Slide a piece of cardboard under the jar to cover the opening.
- Turn the jar over so that the spider falls to the bottom of it.
- Quickly remove the cardboard and put the lid on the jar.

Really, really quickly!

HOW TO AVOID GETTING BITTEN:

- Avoid touching spiders.
- Don't stick your hand into hard to see areas around the garden (behind rotting wood, the dark corner of the shed, holes in the ground etc).
- Wear shoes and gloves when gardening.

DO NOT try to pat or cuddle them!

But spiders aren't all bad.

PEST CONTROL

Spiders are an important part of the ecosystem. They are a form of natural pest control. There are so many spiders . . . so they eat lots of insects, keeping their populations under control. Without spiders, we would be overrun by insects. Of course, spiders also provide food for many animals that prey on them, including birds, lizards and toads.

SPIDERS AS PETS

What's weirder than people keeping snakes as pets? People keeping spiders as pets! Even enormous tarantulas! There are specialty pet stores where you can get them. Well, I suppose if you're not arachnophobic it'd be okay. I suppose some people might think of them as furry and cuddly. BUT NOT ME!

This is me . . . faaaaaaaaar away from the spider.

Australian tarantula

AUSTRALIA'S WEIRDEST SPIDERS:

* Bird-dropping spider (*Celaenia excavata*): Yep! Their bodies looks like lumps of bird poo. It's so birds won't eat them.

* Triangular spiders (*Arkys*): Their bodies are in the shape of a triangle.

* Australian tarantulas (*Theraphosidae*): Also called bird-eating spiders or whistling spiders. The larger ones will hunt for small birds to eat. And they make a hissing/whistling sound with an organ near their mouths, called a lyra.

AUSTRALIA'S CUTEST SPIDER:

* The peacock spider: The male peacock spiders dance around to attract the females. They have become YouTube stars – videos of them dancing have received thousands of views.

Okay, even I think this one is cute.

A big NO from me to ALL spiders. I DO NOT want to meet or touch any of them. Okay, so the peacock spider is kinda cute. And I'm happy to watch YouTube vids of it dancing. But I DO NOT want it dancing on me.

CHAPTER 3

TINY FLYING VAMPIRIC DEATH

You might not think of tiny mosquitoes as being deadly . . . but they can be. Particular types of mosquitoes in certain areas of Australia can carry disease, passing on deadly sicknesses to the people and animals they bite.

AUSTRALIA'S TOP 4 MOSQUITO-BORNE DISEASES

1. Australian encephalitis
2. Dengue fever
3. Ross River virus
4. Barmah Forest virus

BLOODSUCKERS

There are over 300 species of mosquitoes (*Culicidae*) in Australia. The female mosquitoes are the vampires of the insect world and need to FEAST ON BLOOD in order to reproduce. The males usually just feed on nectar.

Name

AUSTRALIAN ENCEPHALITIS

(This covers both Murray Valley encephalitis virus and Kunjin virus)

Symptoms

Mild cases involve fever, loss of appetite and headaches. Severe cases include vomiting, diarrhoea and dizziness, brain dysfunction, lethargy, irritability, drowsiness, confusion, convulsions and fits, coma and death

Other stuff you need to know

● The disease begins in water birds and is then picked up and spread by mosquitoes – particularly *Culex annulirostris* – in the northern areas of Australia.

● The last national epidemic was in 1974 with 58 cases reported and 13 deaths.

FACT FILE

Water birds! It's all their fault! A good reason for eating roast duck. And duck liver pâté, And Peking duck. And duck à l'orange. Now I'm hungry.

FACT FILE

Name
DENGUE FEVER

Symptoms
Fever, severe headaches, and severe pain in the muscles and joints

Other stuff you need to know

- Dengue fever lasts about four to seven days and is usually not fatal. Sometimes, severe cases can lead to Dengue haemorrhagic fever, which involves internal bleeding and can result in death.

- Dengue fever can be transmitted by several different types of mosquito.

- Mosquitoes pick up the disease from infected humans and then pass it on.

> Getting a scratch and bleeding on the outside is bad enough. Bleeding on the inside is best avoided.

FACT FILE

Name
ROSS RIVER VIRUS

Note: Ross River virus is named after the Ross River near Townsville, Queensland, where the virus was first identified.

> I've been there and I didn't get the virus. Phew!

Symptoms
It is often symptomless, but when effects are present they include a rash, mild fever and sometimes arthritis

Other stuff you need to know

- Ross River virus is the most common of the diseases transmitted by mosquitoes. According to the Australian Government Department of Health, 3126 cases were reported in 2018.

- It is transmitted by a number of different mosquitoes in various areas around Australia. Mosquitoes pick it up from native mammals (mostly kangaroos and wallabies) and humans, before transmitting it to other humans.

- Ross River virus is not fatal and mild cases will clear up within a month. Severe cases can last several years with recurring symptoms.

Name

BARMAH FOREST VIRUS

Note: Barmah Forest virus is named after the area it was first discovered, the Barmah Forest in northern Victoria.

Symptoms

It is often symptomless, but when effects are present they include a rash, mild fever, headache, joint pain and swelling, and sometimes arthritis

Other stuff you need to know

● Barmah Forest virus is very similar to, but less common than, Ross River virus. According to the Australian Government Department of Health, in 2018, only 342 cases were reported.

NOT QUITE SO DEAD

JUST DEAD

VERY DEAD

NOT DEAD

VERY **VERY DEAD**

FACT FILE

This mosquito is an *Aedes aegypti*. It can carry dengue fever.

Look at the way this disease-carrying insect vampire is piercing the skin of its victim. It looks just like an injection needle. Aaaagh! If you have a needle-phobia, it would probably be a good idea to NOT LOOK at this photo. Whoops! Too late!

Children's Author Survives Mosquito Attack!

2 April 2015

George Ivanoff, the Australian children's author of popular series such as You Choose and OTHER WORLDS, was attacked by mosquitoes on a recent family holiday.

Travelling from Melbourne to Uluru by car, George and his family stopped to camp at Coward Springs. That evening, while attempting to brush his teeth, he was descended upon by a swarm of ravenous mosquitoes, hungry for his blood. By the time he returned to his tent and found the insect repellent, he had been bitten over 100 times. The following night, staying in Coober Pedy, he was attacked yet again, this time while he slept. The following morning, over 250 mosquito bites covered his body.

George Ivanoff displays the results of the unprovoked mosquito attacks.

'Why me? What did I do to deserve this?' said George. 'I'm just glad I didn't end up getting Dengue fever or some other mosquito-borne virus. OMG! I could have died! I'm never going camping again!'

MOSQUITO SURVIVAL

MOSQUITO BITES RARELY LEAD TO DISEASE. MOST OF THE TIME, THEY ARE JUST IRRITATING. YOU CAN RELIEVE THE ITCHING WITH:

✓ An ice pack.

✓ Special creams or ointments available from a pharmacy.

✓ If you are allergic, you can take a medicine called antihistamine.

BUT THE BEST THING TO DO IS TO NOT GET BITTEN.

✓ Use insect repellent. Note: You can buy insect repellent, or you can spray yourself with mint oil or rub your skin with garlic. But the garlic will probably repel EVERYONE!

✓ Light a citronella candle to keep mosquitoes away.

FUN MOSQUITOES FACTS:

* Mosquitoes are actually a type of fly. There are over 3,000 species worldwide.

* Female mosquitoes live about two to three weeks. Males have even shorter lives.

* A mosquito's saliva stops its victim's blood from clotting.

* Mosquitoes lay their eggs on the surface of stagnant, fresh water.

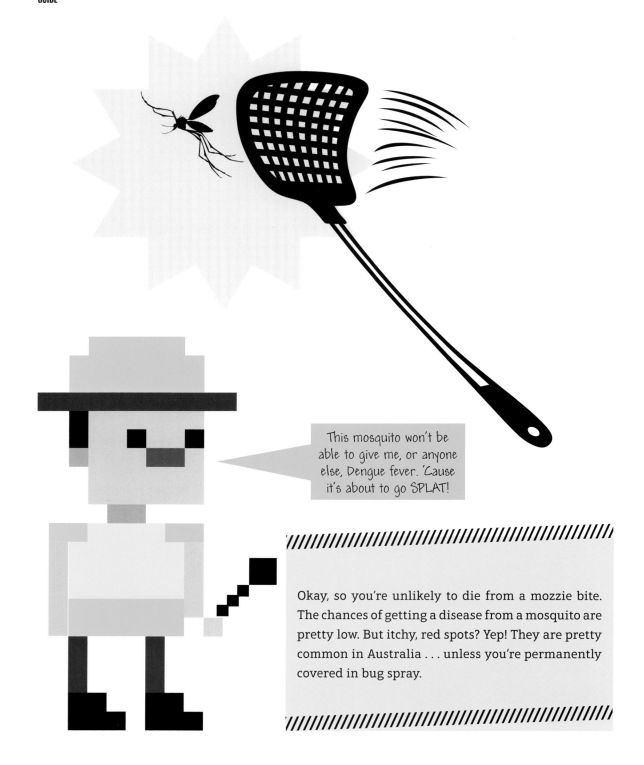

This mosquito won't be able to give me, or anyone else, Dengue fever. 'Cause it's about to go SPLAT!

Okay, so you're unlikely to die from a mozzie bite. The chances of getting a disease from a mosquito are pretty low. But itchy, red spots? Yep! They are pretty common in Australia . . . unless you're permanently covered in bug spray.

CHAPTER 4

TINY NOT-QUITE DEATH

Okay, so this little critter is unlikely to kill you. But it can cause paralysis and is SO GROSS, it earns a place in this guide. In fact . . . it gets its very own chapter. The paralysis tick attaches itself to a host (that could be YOU) and then GORGES ON YOUR BLOOD!

BLOODSUCKING LIFE CYCLE OF A PARALYSIS TICK

Eggs are laid in the ground and they hatch into tiny larvae (0.5 millimetres). The larvae attach themselves to a host and feed. They then drop off and moult, becoming nymphs (2 millimetres). The nymphs attach themselves to a host and feed. Then once again, they drop off and moult, finally becoming adults (4 millimetres). The cycle again repeats and the adults attach themselves to a host. They eventually drop off and reproduce and it all starts over again.

> Horror movie idea – small isolated town is overrun with bloodsucking ticks!

Name

PARALYSIS TICK

Scientific name

Ixodes holocyclus

Location

Coastal areas from eastern Victoria to northern Queensland

Prey

Humans and animals (including domestic pets and marsupials)

Symptoms

Flu-like symptoms, rashes, weakness in limbs, unsteadiness, numbness in limbs and sometimes partial paralysis

Other stuff you need to know

- Young children are most at risk.
- The longer a tick stays attached to its victim, the worse the symptoms.

FACT FILE

- Symptoms of a paralysis tick bite are caused by the tick's saliva.
- A single tick is unlikely to be dangerous to an adult human (unless they're allergic). But multiple bites can cause serious problems.
- Some people are allergic to ticks and will go into anaphylactic shock if bitten.
- No one has died from a paralysis tick bite since 1945.
- Scientists have spent years trying to develop a vaccine, but have so far failed.

> It's just like the bee allergy I told you about on page 25.

Name

PARALYSIS TICK (CONTINUED)
PET DEATH

Paralysis caused by the paralysis tick is not usually a problem for their regular victims, Australian marsupials, as they have developed an immunity. But it is a huge problem for pets. About 10,000–20,000 dogs and cats are paralysed each year and hundreds of them die!

FUN TICK FACTS

* Ticks, along with mites, scorpions and spiders are arachnids.

> OMG! Ticks are related to spiders. No wonder they're so horrible!

* There are about 70 species of ticks in Australia, and they are all bloodsuckers.

BLOOD BAG

> OMG! I think I'm gonna puke!

A paralysis tick can more than double in size while gorging on blood.

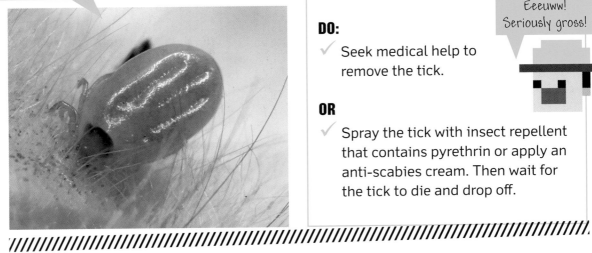

FIRST AID

DO NOT:

✕ Pinch, scratch or try to remove the tick yourself. Removing the tick might break off the creature's mouthpiece while it is still embedded in the skin.

> Eeeuww! Seriously gross!

DO:

✓ Seek medical help to remove the tick.

OR

✓ Spray the tick with insect repellent that contains pyrethrin or apply an anti-scabies cream. Then wait for the tick to die and drop off.

CHAPTER 5

CUTE BUT ~~DEADLY~~ DANGEROUS

Okay . . . these aren't always deadly. But they are dangerous. So even though they're cute . . . DO NOT pat them.

☠ AUSTRALIA'S **TOP 4** CUTE BUT ~~DEADLY~~ DANGEROUS ANIMALS

1. Kangaroo
2. Tasmanian devil
3. Platypus
4. Wombat

Honourable mention: Cassowary – see Fact File to find out why

Name

KANGAROO

Scientific name

There's no scientific name for the grouping known as kangaroos. They are part of a larger group called *Macropus*, which includes wallaroos and some wallabies. Individual species of kangaroo have scientific names. For example, the eastern grey kangaroo is *Macropus giganteus*

Location

Widespread through Australia

Danger

Big claws, powerful hind legs and a strong tail. One of the larger species, such as the eastern grey or red kangaroo (which can get to 2 metres tall), could kill a human being if it attacked. A person is most likely to be kicked to death. But kangaroos attack only if they feel threatened and attacks on humans are rare

Other stuff you need to know

- Kangaroos are marsupials – mammals that carry their young in pouches.
- The collective noun for a group of kangaroos is a mob.
- Kangaroos are fast. Some can reach speeds of 60 kilometres per hour.

Kangaroos are also DELICIOUS! I got to try a kangaroo steak in a restaurant at Uluru.

So don't annoy any large kangaroos.

POSSIBLY DEAD

JUST DEAD

VERY DEAD

NOT QUITE SO DEAD

NOT DEAD

VERY VERY DEAD

FACT FILE

Name

TASMANIAN DEVIL

Scientific name

Sarcophilus harrisii

Location

Tasmania

> Duh! No kidding!

Danger

Powerful jaws and strong teeth. They don't attack humans, but will defend themselves if attacked or trapped

> Okay then . . . so don't attack or trap one, and you should be fine

Other stuff you need to know

- Tasmanian devils are marsupials.
- The '*sarcophilus*' part of its scientific name means 'flesh-lover'.

> Yikes!

- They got their name from the screaming sounds they make.
- Although Tasmanian devils will hunt small animals, they are mostly scavengers, feeding on the bodies of already dead animals.
- Their jaws are powerful enough to crunch through the bones and fur of their food.
- Sadly, Tasmanian devils were declared endangered in 2008.

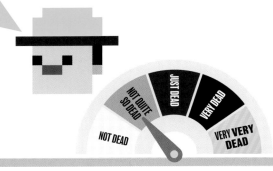

FACT FILE

> It's weird-looking . . . but cute!

Name

PLATYPUS

Scientific name

Ornithorhynchus anatinus

Location

Freshwater areas in Tasmania, the eastern and south-eastern coast of Australia

Danger

Males have a hollow venomous spur on each hind leg. The venom is not deadly to humans, but it can cause severe swelling and lots of pain. They do not attack, but will defend themselves if threatened

Other stuff you need to know

- The platypus is an amphibious, egg-laying mammal belonging to the monotreme group (which includes echidnas).

- When a platypus skin was brought back to England for the first time in 1798, people thought it was a hoax – that someone had sewn a duck's bill and feet to a rabbit skin.
- Platypus bills are electroreceptive. That means they can detect electric currents made by the muscle movements of other creatures in the water. Platypuses use this to navigate under water.

Name
WOMBAT

Scientific name
Vombatidae family

Location
South-eastern and southern Australia, and Tasmania

Danger
Sharp claws and a heavy powerful body (up to 40 kilograms). It doesn't often attack humans, but is dangerous if it does. It can knock a person over and inflict wounds with its claws

Other stuff you need to know
- Like kangaroos and Tassie devils, wombats are marsupials.
- Wombat poo is cube shaped.

FACT FILE

My dad reckons a wombat is like a mini-tank.

NOT QUITE SO DEAD   JUST DEAD   VERY DEAD   NOT DEAD   VERY **VERY DEAD**

Wouldn't it hurt . . . you know . . . coming out?

Cube poo

Wombat Attack:

August 2016

A woman out walking her dogs was viciously attacked by a wombat in the Canberra suburb of Banks, earlier this month. Kerry Evans suffered more than 20 bites and scratches, three of them needing stitches.

Evans was walking along when the wombat charged one of the dogs. The dog tried to run away and Mrs Evans got tangled in the lead and fell over. That's when the wombat attacked her. Every time she tried to get up the creature would bite her and knock her over. Unable to get away from the wombat, she screamed for help.

She was saved by a neighbour and a nearby driver. They came to her aid and the wombat ran away. Paramedics were called and Mrs Evans was taken to hospital.

FACT FILE

Name

SOUTHERN CASSOWARY

Also known as

Double-wattled cassowary

Scientific name

Casuarius casuarius

Location

North-eastern rainforests of Queensland (also in New Guinea and the Aru Islands)

Danger

Powerful legs with a long middle claw on each foot. They will only attack if cornered, but are capable of disembowelling a human with their claws

Other stuff you need to know

- Cassowaries are large flightless birds that are part of the *Ratites* group, which includes emus and ostriches. There are two other species of cassowary living in New Guinea, New Britain and Yapen.

- The bare skin on the heads and necks of southern cassowaries, changes colour with their mood, becoming brighter when they are excited or angry.

- After laying its eggs the female leaves the male to hatch them and raise the chicks.

People don't usually think of these guys as cute, but they need to get a mention.

These things look prehistoric!

Remember – CUTE ≠ SAFE.
Be careful out there!

CHAPTER 6

TOTALLY FAKE DEATH PART 1

You'd think there were enough animals in Australia that could kill you and that we wouldn't need to make any up. But that'd be boring! So, here are some *mythical* animals that could kill you. Well . . . you know . . . if they were real.

AUSTRALIA'S TOP 3 DEADLY MYTHICAL ANIMALS

1. Drop bears
2. *Yara-ma-yha-who*
3. Yowie

Name

DROP BEAR

Origins

Invented as a joke to scare tourists

Other stuff you need to know

- Drop bears are giant carnivorous koalas with sharp teeth, razor-like claws and mean tempers. They live in trees and hunt by dropping onto their victims' heads. Stunned by the impact, victims are usually helpless as they are bitten, clawed and devoured.

- Drop bears hunt at night and will pretty much attack anything that moves, including humans.

- Dabbing Vegemite behind the ears and on the neck is said to ward off drop bears. The best protection, however, is to walk around holding a sharp implement (such as a screwdriver or fork) above the head, so that attacking drop bears are impaled before they can cause harm.

FACT FILE

Aaaagh! I'm glad these things aren't real!

FACT FILE

Name

YARA-MA-YHA-WHO

Origins

Derived from Aboriginal mythology

Other stuff you need to know

- The *yara-ma-yha-who* is a vampiric creature that has the appearance of a small, demon-like man. It is red in colour, has a large head, huge mouth and suckers on its hands and feet.

- It lives in fig trees and will drop down onto its victims. It will suck blood from them, through the suckers on its hands and feet, until the victim becomes unconscious. It will then swallow the victim whole. After having a nap it will regurgitate its prey, still alive, and re-swallow them. It repeats this process until the victim is transformed into a *yara-ma-yha-who*.

That is just too gross for words.

FACT FILE

Name

YOWIE

Origins

Derived from Aboriginal mythology

Other stuff you need to know

- The yowie is Australia's answer to Big Foot and the Abominable Snowman.

- It's a giant ape-like creature that lives in the wilderness. It is between 2.1 and 3.6 metres in height. It has feet that point backwards, making it difficult to track.

- Although thought to be aggressive, there are no records of any humans being attacked.

- There have been many sightings over the years (the first in 1798) but its existence has never been officially proven.

These deadly creatures are not real! So . . . if any of you out there have actually seen one, I want to know about it. 'Cause if we caught one, we could make MILLIONS!

CONCLUSION

Australia has so many land animals that *can* kill you. But, they're not *trying* to kill you. Mostly . . . if you leave them alone, they'll leave you alone.

And there are way more non-dangerous animals than there are dangerous ones. I mean . . . as well as snakes and spiders, Australia also has quokkas, pygmy possums, sugar gliders and bilbies. The off-the-scale cuteness of these animals almost makes up for the deadliness of the dangerous ones.

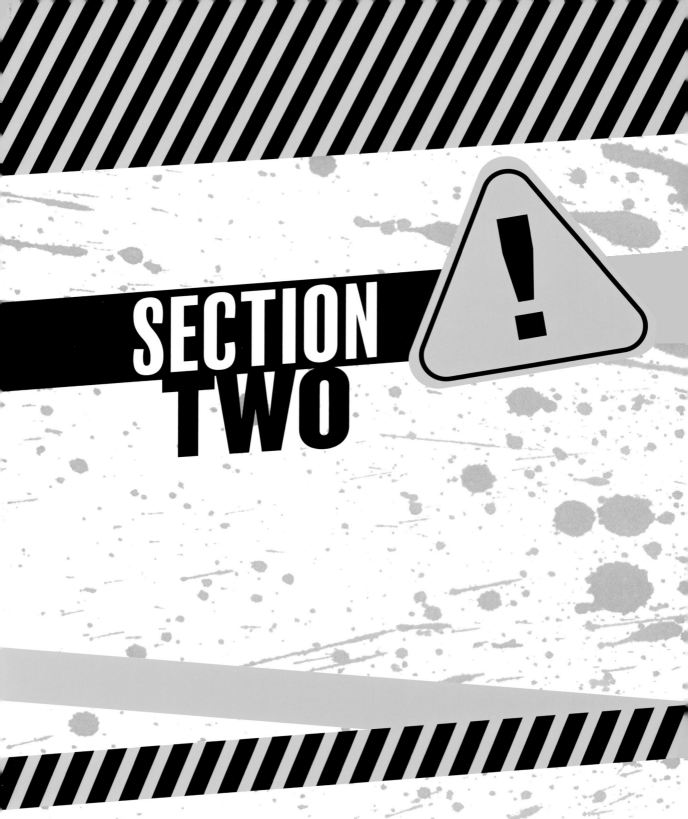

SECTION TWO

IN THE
WATER

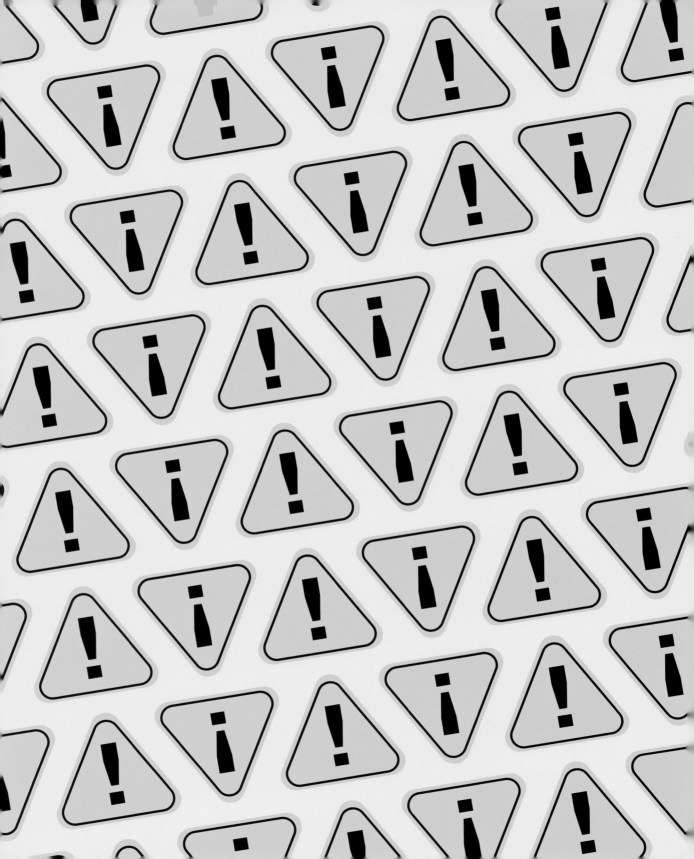

CHAPTER 7

SWIMMING DEATH PART 1

Sharks are fish. Fish with REALLY BIG teeth. Teeth that are REALLY SHARP. These fish want to eat you! These fish want to kill you! Well . . . not really. They just want to eat other marine life. 'Cause they're the oceans' most perfect eating machines. If you get in their way . . . you're in for it! So DON'T get in their way!

There are over 510 different species of shark in the world's oceans, and 182 of them have been seen in Australian waters. AND, we have three of the world's most dangerous sharks!

WHY DO SHARKS ATTACK PEOPLE?

There are a number of different reasons a shark may attack. These include:

- Hunger.
- Curiosity. Sharks are attracted to sounds and bright colours.

> Which means you're just a snack!

- Defence. Sharks can be territorial. If a person gets into a shark's personal space, they may attack.

> Can you imagine it? A shark bites your leg off then says: 'Whoops! Sorry! I thought you were someone else.'

- Mistaken identity. That is, mistaking a human for their normal prey.

ATTACK STATS

* Australia ranks second in the world (behind the USA) for the number of shark attacks.

* The largest number of shark attacks in Australia take place off the coast of New South Wales.

* The largest number of fatal shark attacks in Australia occur off the coast of Western Australia.

> Okay, that's it! I'm never swimming in WA. I'm not even going anywhere near a beach in that state. Heck . . . I don't even want to see pics!

* Between 1988 and 2018, there have been 488 shark attacks in Australia, with 47 of them being fatal.

AUSTRALIA'S TOP 3 DEADLIEST SHARKS

1. Great white shark
2. Tiger shark
3. Bull shark

These three species are responsible for 96 per cent of fatal unprovoked shark attacks in Australia.

FACT FILE

Name

GREAT WHITE SHARK

Also known as

White sharks, white pointer sharks

Scientific name

Carcharodon carcharias

Size

Up to 6 metres

> That's longer than the average car.

Location

North-west cape of Western Australia to southern Queensland and Tasmania

Other stuff you need to know

- Great white sharks are a blue-grey colour with a white underside.

> So . . . great partly-white shark would be a better name.

- The female great white sharks are bigger than the males.
- The worldwide number of great white sharks is steadily getting smaller. This is due to pollution, culling and accidental death caused by being caught in nets.

NOT QUITE SO DEAD · JUST DEAD · VERY DEAD · NOT DEAD · VERY **VERY** DEAD

> So . . . I guess this must be the Great Australian Bite?

Name

TIGER SHARK

Scientific name

Galeocerdo cuvier

Size

Up to 6 metres

Location

Northern Australia from Perth to Sydney

Other stuff you need to know

- Tiger sharks belong to the whaler shark family, as do bull sharks.
- Tiger sharks are grey with a pale underside. Young ones have dark stripes on their backs which can fade as they get older.
- They have hooked teeth.
- They swim closer to shore at night.

FACT FILE

Name

BULL SHARK

Also known as

River whalers

Scientific name

Carcharhinus leucas

Size

Up to 4.2 metres

Location

Northern Australia from Perth to Sydney

Other stuff you need to know

- Bull sharks belong to the whaler shark family, as do tiger sharks.
- They are dark, grey-brown or bronze coloured with a paler underside.
- Bull sharks can inhabit fresh water as well as salt water. They can be found in the rivers and lakes of northern Australia, Western Australia and New South Wales.

FACT FILE

OMG! Isn't it bad enough there are sharks in the ocean without them being in the rivers and lakes AS WELL?

AUSTRALIA'S SUCKIEST SHARK

Whale sharks (*Rhincodon typus*) are fish, not whales. Whale sharks are the largest fish in the ocean, growing up to 18 metres in length, but they only have tiny teeth – less than 6 millimetres. They don't use their teeth for eating. They eat by filtering plankton, krill and small fish. They suck water in through their mouths, then push it out through a filter in their gills. No one's really sure why they have teeth since they don't seem to use them for anything. These gentle sharks are rare and endangered.

OMG! They're like giant swimming vacuum cleaners!

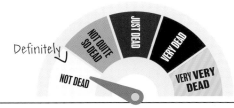

Famous Attacks

One of Australia's most famous shark attacks took place off the coast of South Australia in 1963. While competing in the South Australian Spear Fishing Championship, Rodney Fox was attacked by a great white shark. Although a severe attack, Fox managed to survive. He needed over 400 stitches in his chest, as well as some in his right hand and arm, and extensive rehabilitation for his injuries, which included a punctured lung. Despite being attacked by a shark, Fox became a conservationist, campaigning for the protection of sharks and educating people about their true nature.

What's with 1963? Was it the year of the shark or something?

Actress Marcia Hathaway was killed by a shark in Sydney Harbour in January 1963. Hathaway had only ever appeared in one film, playing a mission nurse in *Shadow of the Boomerang* (1960). She was on a boating trip with her fiancé and their friends, and was wading out into the harbour, just out from Milsons Point, when attacked by the shark. Her fiancé wrestled with the shark to stop it from dragging her under. The shark retreated and Hathaway was pulled from the water, her friends bandaging her wounds while her fiancé swam for help. The ambulance that was sent to get her, broke down along the way and a second one had to be sent for. Sadly, Hathaway died of her injuries before that second ambulance arrived. While she never achieved fame as an actress, Hathaway is remembered as the last person to ever die from a shark attack in Sydney Harbour.

AUSTRALIA'S SMALLEST SHARK

Australia's smallest shark is, in fact, the *world's* second smallest shark – aptly named the pygmy shark (*Euprotomicrus bispinatus*). It grows to only 27 centimetres in length. It spends most of its time in deep water, but will come to the surface after sunset to eat small cephalopods and crustaceans.

Awww! So cute!

Cephalopods! Want to know more? Go look at Chapter 9.

EATING SHARKS

When you order flake from a fish and chips shop, what you're actually eating is . . . shark! In Australia, flake is mostly gummy shark, or sometimes a similar New Zealand species called rig shark.

Ha! Revenge! This is the people's revenge against sharks for all their attacks. Except, of course . . . that this is a different type of shark that doesn't really attack humans. But . . . it's still a shark . . . so . . . REVENGE!

MINIMISING
the risk of
SHARK ATTACK

It's common sense, really. Here are some tips:

✕ Don't go into the water where sharks are known to be.

✕ Do not swim too far from shore.

✓ Swim in areas patrolled by surf lifesavers.

✓ If there is a shark sighting, LEAVE THE WATER as quickly and quietly as possible!

Although there have been some concerns in the past about unsustainable fishing, the Australia government has regulations in place to make sure that gummy sharks are fished sustainably. The only problem with 'flake' is that sometimes other fish are substituted.

Scandal – Fake Flake!

A BAD REP

Sharks have a bad reputation, but they're not as big a threat as people assume. The danger of a shark attack is actually quite low. In Australia, the chances of being bitten by a snake are much higher.

Because sharks have such a bad reputation, there is often a push to cull them. That is, to hunt them to reduce their numbers. Environmentally, this is a BAD THING, since shark populations are already declining. Sharks are also in danger from climate change and the pollution of their habitat. There are over 200 species of shark worldwide listed as threatened, but only three are protected internationally – the great white, whale sharks and basking sharks.

Lots of marine scientists are trying to save shark species from dying out. Check out Shark Conservation Australia: sharkconservation.org.au

FUN SHARK FACTS

* Shark skin feels like sandpaper. *So don't pat them.*

* Different sharks have different shaped teeth. Some are pointed, some are hooked and some are flat.

* Sharks can have up to seven rows of teeth. Whenever they lose or break one, the one behind moves forward to replace it. *Better than going to a dentist!*

* Sharks have a great sense of smell . . . especially for blood!

* Sharks are at the top of the food chain in the ocean. They don't have any predators. *Except humans, I guess.*

Oh man . . . now I feel guilty about eating flake.

I kind of feel sorry for sharks. Movies like *Jaws* make them out to be killing machines that are deliberately out to get people. And that's not the case. They are a necessary part of the oceans' ecosystem, and sometimes, people just get in their way. But people kill more sharks than the other way around. Remember that the next time you eat a piece of flake.

CHAPTER 8

SWIMMING DEATH PART 2

Isn't it bad enough that we have to watch out for sharks when swimming at the beach? No, apparently nowhere near bad enough. We also have to watch out for crocs in the rivers and swamps. These armoured, reptilian creatures look prehistoric. They have BIG mouths and LOTS of teeth. And they are SCARY!!!

THE CROCODILE FAMILY TREE

ORDER	CROCODILIA			
FAMILY	*Cocodylidae*	*Alligatoridae*		*Gavialidae*
SPECIES	**14** species of crocodile (including 2 species in Australia)	**2** species of alligator	**6** species of caiman	**2** species of gharial

All crocodilians are cold-blooded reptiles. They have long snouts with nostrils at the top. This means they can stay underwater, with just the tip of their snouts sticking up out of the water so they can breathe. They all have jaws with sharp conical teeth and have bodies covered in armoured, bony plates.

Crocodiles are the only member of the *crocodilia* order to have V-shaped snouts. When their jaws are closed, crocodiles have more teeth visible, sticking over their bottom and upper lips.

I'm not getting close enough to one of these things to work out if it's a crocodile or an alligator or a whatever!

AUSTRALIA'S
TOP 2
DEADLIEST CROCODILES

1. Estuarine crocodiles
2. Freshwater crocodiles

> Actually, they are Australia's ONLY crocs. But that doesn't stop them being deadly.

FACT FILE

Name

ESTUARINE CROCODILES

Also known as

Saltwater crocodile

Scientific name

Crocodylus porosus

Size

5–7 metres

Habitat

Coastal rivers, creeks, estuaries and swamps

> That's longer than a great white shark, which is longer than a car.

Location

Northern coastal areas in Western Australia, Northern Territory and Queensland

Prey

Mammals, birds and fish. They will eat almost anything that comes close enough, including humans

Other stuff you need to know

● Australia's most dangerous crocodile.

● Estuarine crocodiles come in a range of colours from grey to brown to almost black, with darker mottled patterns.

● They are the world's largest reptile.

● These crocodiles are found in many parts of the world.

● They swallow their smaller prey whole. But they'll drag larger prey under the water and do a 'death roll', twisting it around until it dies. Then they will rip it to pieces.

> Death roll? OMG! It's called a death roll!

NOT QUITE SO DEAD · JUST DEAD · VERY DEAD · NOT DEAD · VERY VERY DEAD

ATTACK STATS

* Between 1865 and 2018, there have been a total of 233 reported crocodile attacks, 82 of which were fatal. The majority of attacks were by estuarine crocodiles. Only 22 of the attacks were by freshwater crocodiles, none of which were fatal.

* For more statistics check out the CrocBITE: Worldwide Crocodilian Attack Database: crocodile-attack.info

---

Name

FRESHWATER CROCODILE

Also known as
Johnstone's crocodile

Scientific name
Crocodylus johnstoni

Size
Up to 3 metres

Habitat
Rivers, swamps and billabongs

Location
Northern areas in Western Australia, Northern Territory and Queensland

Prey
Fish, frogs, lizards, snakes, birds and small mammals.

Other stuff you need to know
● Australia's second-most dangerous crocodile.

● Freshwater crocodiles are grey to brown with darker bands.

● They don't normally attack humans. But they can be attracted to movement in the water, so swimmers are at risk of injury. Also, people dangling their feet in the water over the sides of boats run the risk of being bitten.

● These crocodiles are not found anywhere else in the world.

FACT FILE

You could end up without feet to dangle if you're not careful.

Well, there are only two types in Australia. So, I guess you could also say it's Australia's least-dangerous crocodile.

Poke it in the Eye

October 1990

A woman was saved from a crocodile attack by her son, who scared the creature off by poking it in the eyes.

Camping near Woodycupaldiya, on the Western Australia-Northern Territory border, the Pangquee family set up their tent next to a creek known for its barramundi. Little did they realise that their choice of location would lead to a terrifying encounter.

During the night, the family were woken by a 4-metre long croc ripping through the mesh of their tent. Fifty-five-year-old Lena Pangquee, threw herself between the croc and her husband, who had recently suffered a stroke and was still recovering. The croc grabbed her around the chest with its jaws.

Lena's thirty-five-year-old son, Peter, sprang into action, sticking his fingers into the croc's eyes. The creature immediately released Lena and headed back to the water.

Lena was taken to Royal Darwin Hospital to recover from her injuries.

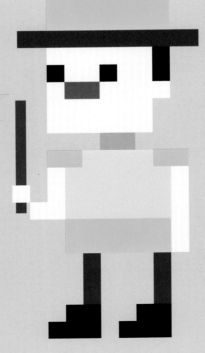

If I was going to poke a croc in the eye, I'd use a stick.

CROCODILE SAFETY

HOW TO AVOID A CROC ATTACK

✕ DO NOT enter or approach water in a known crocodile-inhabited area. There are usually signs!

✓ If you are uncertain about an area CHECK with the local authorities, local government office or tourist centre.

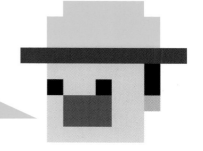

This is not hard. Anyone can avoid a croc attack by following these simple instructions.

FUN CROC FACTS

* Crocodiles are unable to sweat.

> So I guess that means they don't need deodorant.

* They are really good at holding their breath and can stay under water for long periods of time.

* Crocodiles tire easily. So after eating or fighting, they need to rest.

* Crocodiles have really strong muscles to close their jaws, but really weak muscles for opening their jaws. So, closing their mouths, they are strong enough to crush the bones and skull of their prey. But a strong rubber band around the snout is enough to keep their jaws shut.

> Additional survival tip – always keep a rubber band in your pocket.

CROCODILE SKINS

In the past, crocodiles in Australia were intensely hunted for their skins. In fact, they were in danger of becoming extinct. They were listed as protected in the 1960s and 70s, with crocodile numbers increasing since then. These days, only farmed crocodiles are the source of leather in Australia. Crocodile leather is popular for products such as wallets, bags and belts.

> I got to visit a croc farm in Queensland with my parents. And I got to eat a croc-burger! But I decided against getting a croc-wallet.

EATING CROCODILES

Crocodile meat is a gourmet item in restaurants around the world. The meat is low in fat and cholesterol, but high in protein, so it's a healthy choice. Crocodiles in Australia are protected, so crocodile meat comes from farmed animals, not those in the wild. The taste is described as a cross between chicken and fish.

> I'm getting hungry.

Crocodiles are a bit like sharks really, in that they have a bad rep. But like sharks, they are a necessary part of ecosystem. Still, many people think they should be culled in order to keep humans safe. But humans can stay safe simply by keeping out of their way. It's not a case of humans versus crocs. Australia is a BIG country. I'm sure we can share it.

CHAPTER 9

TENTACLED DEATH

It's small! It's cute! It's DEADLY!

You don't normally think of octopuses killing people . . . except for giant, boat-crushing ones in sci-fi stories. But blue-ringed octopuses *can* kill people. In fact, they're the only octopuses known to be deadly to humans. And we've got them in Australian waters.

OCTOPUSES

Octopuses are molluscs, which are soft, boneless animals. Some molluscs, such as snails, clams and oysters, have shells to protect them, but others, such as slugs and octopuses do not. Octopuses, along with squids, nautiluses and cuttlefishes, fall into the cephalopod grouping.

Octopuses use their arms to walk on the ocean floor. They swim by pumping water out through a tube in their bodies, called a siphon.

There are over 250 species of octopus that range from under 2.5 centimetres to 8 metres in length, with their arms stretched out. There are about 50 species that live in Australian waters. Of these, the blue-ringed octopus is the one to avoid.

A person who studies octopuses is called a cephalopodiatrist (actually, they also study squids and nautiluses).

SHOCK! HORROR! I don't believe it! Octopuses DO NO have tentacles. They are actually called ARMS not TENTACLES. A squid has tentacles, but an octopus has arms. Calling them tentacles is a MISTAKE. But everyone does it. Well . . . everyone except octopus experts. Hmmm! Should I rename this chapter ARMED DEATH?

FACT FILE

Name

BLUE-RINGED OCTOPUS

(there are three species in Australia)

Scientific name

Hapalochlaena maculosa (southern blue-ringed octopus); *Hapalochlaena fasciata* (blue-lined octopus); *Hapalochlaena lunulata* (greater blue-ringed octopus)

> I don't think I can pronounce any of these.

Size

Up to 20 centimetre arm-span, depending on the species

Habitat

Bottom of the ocean to a depth of 30 metres

Location

The southern blue-ringed octopus around southern Australia coasts; the blue-lined octopus in New South Wales and Queensland, and the greater blue-ringed octopus along northern coasts

Prey

Crabs, shrimp and fish

Effects of venom

Muscle weakness, nausea, difficulty swallowing, difficulty breathing and paralysis.

Other stuff you need to know

- They have rings and lines of blue colour on their bodies. The rings are usually pale, but glow vividly when they become agitated.

- They have strong mouths with a bird-like beak, which is located on the underside of their bodies.

- They can change colour to blend in with their surrounds. If attacked, they will show their blue rings as a warning before biting.

> Sneaky!

- The blue-ringed octopus also lives in other parts of the world.

- They spend most of their time in a lair – a crack in a rock, a cave-like hole in a coral reef or sometimes they'll use an abandoned shell or an empty can.

> It makes them sound like evil super-villains, with hidden underwater lairs.

NOT QUITE SO DEAD · JUST DEAD · VERY DEAD · NOT DEAD · VERY VERY DEAD

FUN OCTOPUS FACTS

* Octopuses have three hearts.

* Their blood is blue because it contains a copper-based protein called hemocyanin.

* They squirt ink.

* They can regrow lost arms.

* They have been around a long time – about 296 million years.

* Octopus is a popular food in many countries, including Japan, Spain and Greece.

BLUE-RINGED OCTOPUS BITE

People often don't feel the bite, so don't realise there is a problem until they begin to exhibit symptoms. Blue-ringed octopuses are not aggressive. Most bites happen when people pick them up, not realising what they are, or accidentally step on them because they're camouflaged.

They are one of the most venomous marine animals in the world.

Like I said before . . . they are SNEAKY!

Lots of things I've read say that, even though there have been lots of people bitten by blue-ringed octopuses, only two people have died in Australia from the bites. So they're not all bad. Mind you, about the only other nice thing to say about these little guys is that they're pretty.

There is no antivenom, so a victim needs to be treated for the symptoms until the venom wears off. Even though paralysed, victims are usually conscious. Victims need to be given CPR if they stop breathing. In severe cases they may need to be put on a respirator (a machine that breathes for them). The venom usually wears off within 24 hours.

OMG! NO ANTIVENOM!

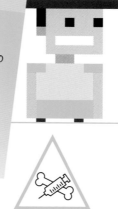

CPR

X CPR stands for cardiopulmonary resuscitation. It involves chest compressions (pressing down on the chest over the heart) to make the heart beat, and rescue breaths (breathing into the victim's mouth) to get air into their lungs.

Lucky Escape

21 February 2018

A young boy is lucky to have escaped unscathed from a playful encounter with a deadly blue-ringed octopus at a beach in Adelaide.

Out for a day at Somerton Beach with his mother, eight-year-old Noah found a tiny, cute octopus hidden inside a shell he had picked up in his net. He poked it with his fingers, then he brought it over to his mum and proudly showed her what he had caught.

His mother recognised the blue rings, which became quite vivid and took the creature away. It was a lucky escape for Noah, as the bite of a blue-ringed octopus is extremely dangerous.

He tried to play with a blue-ringed octopus? They're not TOYS!

One of these is a toy.
The other is a DEADLY sea creature.
DO NOT mix them up!

FIRST AID

DO:

- ✓ Call 000 immediately.
- ✓ Keep the victim as still and calm as possible.
- ✓ Use a pressure immobilisation bandage. (This is a bandage that wraps an entire limb tightly and also has a splint to stop it from moving.)
- ✓ If the victim is having trouble breathing, administer CPR until an ambulance arrives.

DO NOT:

- ✗ DO NOT apply a tourniquet.
- ✗ DO NOT cut the wound.
- ✗ DO NOT try to suck out the venom.

HOW TO AVOID BEING BITTEN

- ✗ DO NOT pick up any octopuses . . . ever!
- ✗ DO NOT swim on beaches where there are warning signs.
- ✗ If exploring rock pools, DO NOT stick your fingers into any holes or crevices in the rocks.

SMALLEST OCTOPUS IN THE WORLD

The star-sucker pygmy octopus (*Octopus wolfi*), is the tiniest octopus in the world. It is less than 2.5 centimetres in length and weighs less than a gram.

BIGGEST OCTOPUS IN THE WORLD

The giant Pacific octopus (*Enteroctopus dofleini*) is the world's largest octopus. It grows to about 5 metres in length and can weigh up to 50 kilograms.

It's also the cutest octopus in the world. Pity it doesn't live around Australia. This is one that I'd actually like to meet. And it could hang out with the peacock spider (see page 34). That would break every known cuteness record.

CHAPTER 10

WIBBLY-WOBBLY JELLY DEATH

They're called jellyfish. But they're not fish! And they're not made of jelly! How tricky is that? They're also really into stinging, with toxic venom. I don't like them!

JELLYFISH

Although they are not made of jelly, they are jelly-like, which is how they got their name. Their bodies are shaped like umbrellas and mostly made up of water. The umbrella-shaped body is called a bell. Below the bell, they have tentacles that they use to sting and catch prey. Their mouths are at the bottom of their bells.

Jellyfish do not have lungs like land animals, or gills like fish – they breathe through the thin outer layer of their skins. Many jellyfish have such thin skins that they are see-through.

The stinging cells on their tentacles are called nematocysts and each contains a venom-filled dart.

There are over 2,000 species of jellyfish and they belong to one of the most common groups of sea animals – *Cnidaria*.

Jellyfish are found in oceans all over the world.

BLOOMING

Sometimes jellyfish will gather together in large groups. This is called a bloom. There can be as many as 100,000 of them in a bloom.

That's a bit bloomin' freaky.

MOUTHS

Jellyfish have only one opening on their bodies – a mouth. They eat with their mouths. But they also expel waste through their mouths.

Oh, that is GROSS! That means POO and WEE, doesn't it? Through. Their. Mouths!

AUSTRALIA'S TOP 3 VENOMOUS JELLYFISH

1. Box jellyfish
2. Irukandji jellyfish
3. Common bluebottle jellyfish

FACT FILE

Common name

BOX JELLYFISH

Also known as

Sea wasps

Scientific name

Chironex fleckeri

Size

Up to 38 centimetres (width of bell), but their tentacles can extend up to 3 metres

Habitat

Warm river mouths and shallow coastal waters

Location

Northern coasts of Queensland, Northern Territory and Western Australia

Prey

Shrimp, fish, crustaceans, worms, other jellyfish

Effects of venom

Intense pain, swelling and redness in sting area, difficulty breathing and cardiac arrest

> That means your heart STOPS BEATING!

Other stuff you need to know

- Box jellyfish have a box-like body, with four flattened sides and a rounded top.

- There are many species of box jellyfish, all grouped together in the class *Cubozoa*. The *Chironex fleckeribox* jellyfish is the most deadly.

> Read the signs, people!

- Deadly box jellyfish have up to 15 stinging tentacles that hang down from each of the four corners of their box.

> That's 60 STINGING TENTACLES in total!

- Summer is the danger period as winds and currents can bring them close to shore. Signs on Queensland beaches warn people when not to swim.

FACT FILE

Common name

IRUKANDJI JELLYFISH

Also known as

Marine stingers

Scientific name

There are 16 species of Irukandji jellyfish, the best known being *Carukia barnesi* and *Malo kingi*

Size

Up to 2.5 centimetre (width of bell)

> That's about the size of a $2 coin.

Habitat

Deep, warm offshore waters

Location

Off the coast of Queensland, the Northern Territory and Western Australia

Prey

Zooplankton, small crustaceans, small fish

Effects of venom

Lower backache, headache, muscle cramps and pain, pain in chest and abdomen, nausea, vomiting and breathing difficulties. Severe cases can include heart failure, fluid on the lungs and brain haemorrhage

> That's when your heart can't pump enough blood around your body.

> That's an exploding artery in the brain that causes bleeding, which KILLS brain cells. Yikes!

Other stuff you need to know

● Irukandji jellyfish are the world's smallest jellyfish.

● Irukandji jellyfish belong to the box jellyfish class *Cubozoa*.

● The effects of the Irukandji jellyfish venom is called Irukandji syndrome. Death from Irukandji syndrome is rare, but the syndrome is severe and usually results in hospitalisation. It is excruciatingly painful.

> Ouch!

● Irukandji jellyfish are almost invisible in the water because their skin is transparent and they're so small. They have only four tentacles but there are nematocysts on their body as well as on their tentacles.

● The peak season for these jellyfish coming close to shore is November to May.

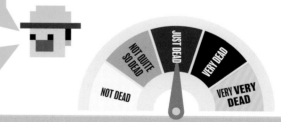

NOT QUITE SO DEAD · JUST DEAD · VERY DEAD · NOT DEAD · VERY VERY DEAD

> In 2002, research scientist Robert King died from *Malo kingi* stings while snorkelling in Queensland. The species was named after him and nicknamed the common kingslayer.

> Oh! I thought it might be because these jellyfish went around killing royal people.

Okay, so the common bluebottle jellyfish is not deadly to humans. But it stings more people in Australia than any other jellyfish, so I thought I should include it. Plus, it is really WEIRD!

FACT FILE

Common name

COMMON BLUEBOTTLE JELLYFISH

Also known as

Pacific man-of-war

Scientific name

Physalia utriculus

Size

Up to 15 centimetres (width of float)

Habitat

Warm tropical waters

Location

Eastern coast of Australia, southern coast of Western Australia

Prey

Plankton and small crustaceans

Effects of venom

Redness and swelling around sting, pain around sting

Other stuff you need to know

- The stings of the common bluebottle jellyfish are not deadly to humans (unless you are unlucky enough to be allergic), and the effects usually wear off within 30 minutes to an hour.

- Winds and currents bring them closer to shore during the summer months on the eastern coast of Australia, and during autumn and winter in southern Western Australia.

- Common bluebottle jellyfish are different from other jellyfish. They are colony organisms called siphonophores. There is one main organism, the float or bottle (like the bell on an ordinary jellyfish), which is a blue pear-shaped sac, with other smaller organisms attached to it. They are dependent on each other and together they form the common bluebottle jellyfish. Even the tentacles are separate organisms. These separate organisms are call zooids.

This sounds more like some bizarre alien creature from a sci-fi film than a jellyfish.

- People often confuse them with the larger Portuguese man-of-war, which is found in the Atlantic Ocean.

Common bluebottle jellyfish are the UNDERCOVER SPIES of the ocean. Even though they're referred to as jellyfish, they are not actually true jellyfish. They are zooids in disguise!

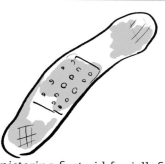

FIRST AID

Administering first aid for jellyfish stings can be confusing and sometimes even the experts don't agree on what you should do. A lot depends on the sort of jellyfish you've been stung by.

DO:

✓ For box jellyfish and Irukandji jellyfish, pour vinegar onto sting area for 30 seconds. (This will neutralise any remaining stinging cells.) If vinegar is not available, wash the area with sea water (not fresh water).

✓ For bluebottle jellyfish, immerse the sting area in hot water. (But not too hot, as you don't want to scald the skin). A hot bath or shower will work. Do not use vinegar.

✓ Get medical help.

✓ Keep the victim as still and calm as possible.

✓ If the victim is not breathing, administer CPR until an ambulance arrives.

DO NOT:

✕ DO NOT apply methylated spirits or any kind of alcohol. (It may make the sting worse.)

✕ DO NOT pee on the sting site. This is an urban myth. It does not help!

✕ DO NOT use a compression bandage.

> Ew! I've never heard of this urban myth. What would make anyone think that peeing on a sting would help?

HOW TO AVOID GETTING STUNG:

✓ Swim at patrolled beaches.

✓ DO NOT swim on beaches where signs warn of jellyfish danger.

✓ Wear a 'stinger suit' made of lycra or neoprene.

EATING JELLY

So, it turns out you can eat jellyfish. They are really high in protein but low in fat. Not many people in Australia eat them, but they have been enjoyed in China for hundreds of years, often used in salads or eaten pickled. There are about 30 edible species of jellyfish.

The jellyfish population is on the increase and, in fact, there is a danger of over population. Perhaps the solution is to eat them?

> I think I'd rather eat raspberry jelly.

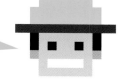

STINGER SUITS

Want to go swimming with jellyfish?

Want protection from sunburn?

Want to feel safe in the water?

Protect yourself with the
STING-NO-MORE Stinger Suit.

Say goodbye to **BOX JELLYFISH**
and **IRUKANDJI JELLYFISH** stings.

This Stinger Suit could save your life!

Made from quality fade-resistant lycra.

Order now for just $99.99!

I think I'll just avoid
swimming near jellyfish.

Lifesavers to the Rescue!

September 2015

Brendan, a Darwin boy, was stung by a deadly box jellyfish . . . while at a kids' lifesaving session!

The young boy was 50 metres out from shore when he was stung on the arm by a box jellyfish. But since he was at a lifesaving event, there was no shortage of people to rescue him.

He was quickly brought to shore, where lifesavers poured vinegar over the sting area. He was then given oxygen until an ambulance arrived to take him to hospital. Luckily it was a minor sting, so all he needed was some medication to help with the pain.

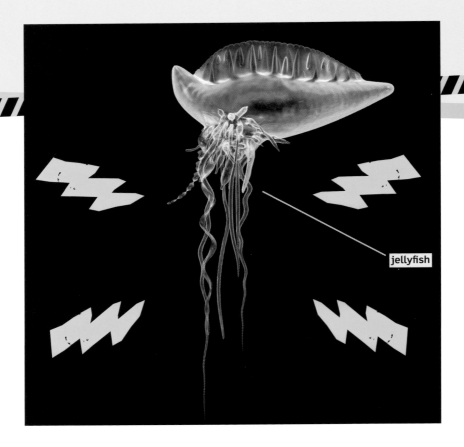

jellyfish

MEDICAL RESEARCH

Jellyfish have been a big help in medical research. The green fluorescent protein from crystal jellyfish (*Aequorea victoria*) have been used in the study of Alzheimer's disease. Jellyfish are also being used in cancer research. The toxins of various jellyfish, including the box jellyfish are being examined for their anti-cancer effects.

Mum and dad took me to an aquarium on our trip. They had some jellyfish in tanks. I spent ages just watching them floating around. I've gotta say that some of them are a bit . . . beautiful. Dad used the words 'elegant' and 'graceful' to describe them. And I guess he's right. But while I'm happy to look at them in aquariums, I reckon I'm gonna keep my distance from them out in the wild.

CHAPTER 11

TOTALLY FAKE DEATH PART 2

There seems to be quite a lot of mythical animals around . . .

In the previous section, I listed the mythical land animals. Now here are some water creatures . . .

AUSTRALIA'S TOP 2 DEADLY MYTHICAL WATER CREATURES

1. Bunyip
2. Hawkesbury River Monster

FACT FILE

Name

BUNYIP

Origin

Derived from Aboriginal legends and possibly gets its origins from the prehistoric marsupial diprotodon

Other stuff you need to know

● Bunyips are Australia's most famous monsters. They live in billabongs, swamps and waterholes.

● Descriptions of this creature vary wildly, so no one is 100 per cent sure what they look like. Does it have feathers and fins, tusks and claws, one eye or a mouth in its stomach? Your guess is as good as mine. The one thing most accounts agree on is the loud howling, screeching sounds that bunyips make. They hunt at night, coming out of their watery homes to feed on animals and small children. There have been many sightings over the years, especially in the 1930s, but no evidence of their existence has been found.

Do not get these guys to babysit. It will not end well.

FACT FILE

Name

HAWKESBURY RIVER MONSTER

Origin

Derived from Aboriginal legends

Other stuff you need to know

- The Hawkesbury River Monster is Australia's answer to the Loch Ness Monster. It lives in the Hawkesbury River in New South Wales, and looks like a prehistoric plesiosaur. In fact, many monster hunters insist it is a plesiosaur that has somehow survived extinction. There have been many sightings, but scientific studies of the river have failed to gather any evidence. The Hawkesbury River is a popular tourist destination and stories of the monster seem to encourage tourists to visit.

I think I've solved the mystery of the Hawkesbury River Monster. I reckon it's a government conspiracy to increase tourism.

NOT QUITE SO DEAD · JUST DEAD · VERY DEAD · NOT DEAD · VERY **VERY DEAD**

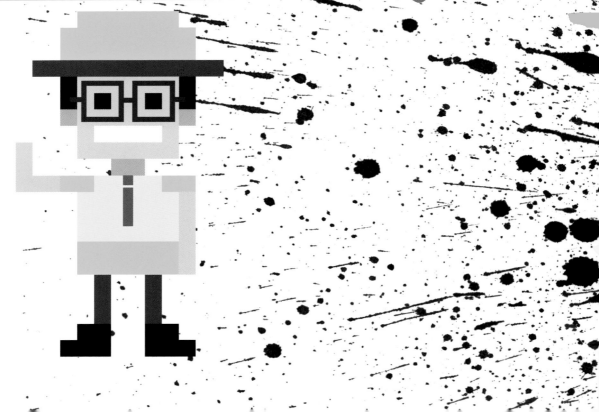

CONCLUSION

There are lots of deadly creatures in Australia's waters. But staying safe is all about being sensible. You can avoid dying! And if you can avoid dying, you can sit back, relax and enjoy Australia's awesome marine life.

There is so much amazing stuff in the water. It's not all dangerous. And even the dangerous stuff serves a purpose. Sharks and crocs and other dangerous creatures are part of the ecosystem. And even though they can be dangerous to humans, they are also MAGNIFICENT! And jellyfish are being used in medical research.

So I guess . . . DANGEROUS ≠ BAD. These creatures are not super villains, plotting your downfall. They are just trying to survive.

Stay out of their way. Appreciate them from a distance.

And you can get closer to the other, less dangerous, water-dwellers. Things like feather stars (*crinoids*), which look like walking plants, and the wondrous sea butterfly (*corolla ovate*) are just unbelievably amazing.

SECTION THREE

THE
ENVIRONMENT

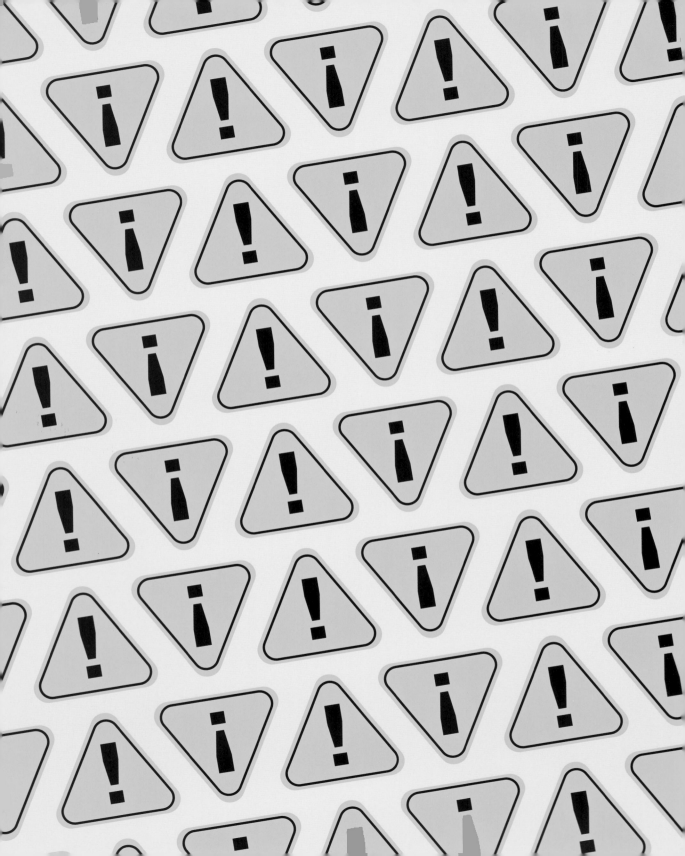

CHAPTER 12

HOT THIRSTY DEATH

Imagine wandering through a desolate, endless sea of sand. Hot sun mercilessly beating down on you. No hat. No water. Snakes trying to bite you. Mobs of kangaroos trying to run you down. You wouldn't last long, would you? You'd soon be DEAD! Deserts . . . they're Australia's DEATHTRAPS! And so much of this country is covered in deserts . . . or places that are almost deserts.

Desert

noun

a waterless, desolate area of land with little or no vegetation.

Desert not dessert

You really don't want to get these mixed up. Desserts are yummy. You want as many as you can get into your mouth. Deserts are not yummy. They're kind of sandy and gritty and not all that great when you put a spoonful in your mouth.

Dessert

Desert

AUSTRALIA'S
TOP 10
DESERTS
FROM BIGGEST TO SMALLEST

The Australian Bureau of Statistics classifies over two thirds of Australia as being arid or semi-arid. Within the arid regions, there are ten deserts.

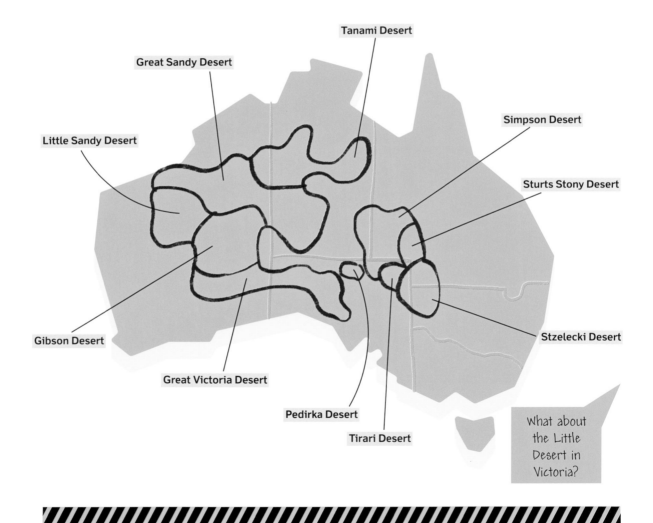

Tanami Desert

Great Sandy Desert

Simpson Desert

Little Sandy Desert

Sturts Stony Desert

Gibson Desert

Stzelecki Desert

Great Victoria Desert

Pedirka Desert

Tirari Desert

What about the Little Desert in Victoria?

1. Great Victoria Desert
Western Australia/South Australia
Approximately 348,750 kilometres^2

2. Great Sandy Desert
Western Australia/Northern Territory
Approximately 284,993 kilometres^2

3. Tanami Desert
Northern Territory/Western Australia
Approximately 184,500 kilometres^2

4. Simpson Desert
Northern Territory/South Australia/
Queensland
Approximately 176,500 kilometres^2

5. Gibson Desert
Western Australia
Approximately 156,000 kilometres^2

6. Little Sandy Desert
Western Australia
Approximately 110,900 kilometres^2

7. Strzelecki Desert
South Australia/Queensland/New
South Wales
Approximately 80,250 kilometres^2

8. Sturts Stony Desert
South Australia/Queensland
Approximately 29,750 kilometres^2

9. Tirari Desert
South Australia
Approximately 15,250 kilometres^2

10. Pedirka Desert
South Australia
Approximately 1250 kilometres^2

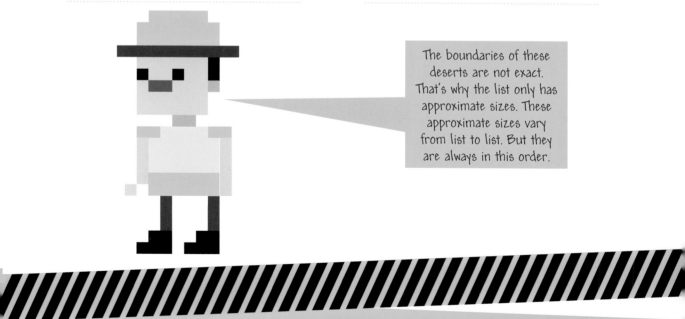

The boundaries of these deserts are not exact. That's why the list only has approximate sizes. These approximate sizes vary from list to list. But they are always in this order.

Getting Lost!

The conditions in Australian deserts are harsh. Daytime temperatures are usually above 35°C in summer and night-time temperatures in winter are often 3–6°C, although some areas can head into the negative degrees. Getting stranded or lost in a desert is dangerous and potentially life-threatening. Each year this is what happens to many tourists . . . and some of them even die.

Always plan carefully when visiting desert areas.

LITTLE DESERT NATIONAL PARK

The Little Desert in Victoria is not little and it's not a desert. At over 1300 kilometres^2 it is actually bigger than the Pedirka Desert. Even though it's called 'The Little Desert', it gets too much rain to be officially classified as a desert.

TOP TEMPERATURE

Australia's highest temperature of 50.7°C was recorded on 2 January 1960 in Oodnadatta in South Australia. Oodnadatta is a town surrounded by cattle farms and is situated near the Simpson Desert.

AUSTRALIA'S HOTTEST DESERT

Australia's hottest area is the Pilbara region in Western Australia. The Great Sandy Desert is partly in this region. Summer temperatures there can reach 48–50°C.

But Australia's highest temperature wasn't recorded in a desert . . .

RAIN IN THE DESERT

Australian deserts get an average rainfall of less than 250 millimetres a year. In comparison, Sydney has an average yearly rainfall of over 1000 millimetres.

I'm getting thirsty just thinking about it.

AUSTRALIA'S TOP 4 DESERT DANGERS

1. Hot during the day
2. Cold at night
3. Lack of water
4. Huge area to get lost in

DESERT DEATHS

So many reported deaths over the years. I just can't read them all. It's too gruesome!

Family Found in Desert

November 2018
The bodies of two adults and one [...] their broken down car in a remote part of ce[...] was found 120m from the others [...] extreme heat.

Desert Trek Turns to Disaster

April 2005
Two men and their dog have been found dead in the Gibson Desert. They were driving to Halls Creek, when their Land Rover broke down. Police said that the vehicle was in poor condition for such a trip, and that the men didn't have enough water or petrol for their journey. They also neglected to tell anyone of their travel plans.

Simpson Des[...] Tragedy

December 1963
The Page family was crossi[...] Desert when their car ran [...] the Birdsville track. All five [...] died from heat and dehyd[...] decided to leave the car and walk.

NOT DEAD · NOT QUITE SO DEAD · JUST DEAD · VERY DEAD · VERY VERY DEAD

SURVIVAL TIPS

- ✓ Always make sure someone knows where you are going and when you are due to arrive at your destination.
- ✓ Travel with plenty of water.
- ✓ Carry a compass and a map.
- ✓ Dress for the heat in lightweight clothing with long sleeves and always wear a hat.
- ✓ Do not stray from roads and paths. If stranded, stay with your vehicle and wait to be rescued.
- ✓ If you get lost, seek shade from the sun during the day and find shelter at night to escape the cold, even if it is just huddling under some bushes.
- ✓ Conserve energy . . . do not wander about aimlessly. If you need to travel, do so at night when it is cooler.
- ✓ If you don't have water with you, try to find moisture. The roots of some mallee plants and wattles can contain water. As a last resort, you could drink your own urine.

Eew! Gross!

- ✓ If lost, create signals to help rescuers find you. Spell out SOS in rocks, and at night light a campfire .

Should I drink my own wee?

Only in extreme situations! Healthy urine contains about 95 per cent water and is sterile. BUT . . .

- 5 per cent is made up of waste filtered out by your kidneys, including urea, chloride and potassium. These will go back into your body when you drink the urine and put extra strain on your kidneys.
- If you have a kidney infection, your wee is no longer sterile and will contain harmful bacteria.
- The more (dehydrated) you are, the less water is in your wee.
- The more times you drink your wee, the less water will be in the next lot. So . . .

Only drink your wee if there is no other option. But remember: if you have reached the point where you are ready to drink your own wee, chances are you are already dehydrated.

Hmmm. Good point!

Grandmother Survives the Australian Outback

June 2015

South Australian grandmother, Cheryl Redway, 64, survived alone in the Great Sandy Desert for over two days, before being found by rescuers.

Mrs Redway and her husband were on holiday, camping at the Salt Creek rest area, 80 kilometres from King's Canyon in the Northern Territory's Great Sandy Desert. Taking a morning walk, Mrs Redway became disorientated and lost. When she failed to return to the campsite, rescuers were called in and a search mounted. Helicopters, motorcycles and trackers were used in the search, and Mrs Redway was eventually found, over two days later, only 2.5 kilometres from the campsite.

Mrs Redway survived temperatures below 5°C at night by huddling down in some bushes. But she had no protection from the heat of the day and did not have any water with her. Her survival was very lucky, indeed.

Life in the Desert

People often associate deserts with lifelessness, but Australian deserts are homes for a large variety of plant and animal life. Many species have adapted to the harsh conditions. Mulga bushes and spinifex grasses are the most common of desert plants. A wide variety of reptiles, birds, mammals, frogs and insects also inhabit Australian deserts. In fact, Aussie deserts have the largest variety of lizard life of all the world's deserts.

So I guess the deserts aren't deserted. LOL!

FACT BOX

Name

THORNY DEVIL

Scientific name

Moloch horridus

Size

Up to 20 centimetres in length

Habitat

Desert areas

Prey

Ants

I met one of these lizards while we were in the Simpson Desert. DO NOT pick them up. They are spiky! But they are kinda cute.

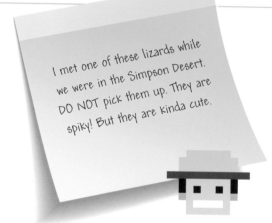

DESERT PEOPLE

Today, less than 3 per cent of Australia's population live in desert regions. But Indigenous Australians have inhabited desert areas for thousands of year. There are still Aboriginal communities living in desert areas. The Pila Nguru (also known as the Spinifex People) live in one of Australia's most remote communities, 10 kilometres north-west of Tjuntjuntjara, Western Australia, in the Great Victoria Desert. These people have lived in the area for more than 15,000 years.

Visit the Big Rock

Uluru (also known as Ayers Rock) is one of Australia's greatest landmarks and biggest tourist attractions. Located in the Northern Territory, it is situated west of the Simpson Desert. Uluru is over 600 million years old. It is approximately 3.6 kilometres long and 1.9 kilometres wide, with a circumference of 9.4 kilometres around the base. The walk around the rock can be completed in about three and a half hours. Its red-orange appearance is due to the oxidisation of the iron in the rock. Tourist brochures will often claim that Uluru is the world's largest single rock or monolith. It's not. It is actually part of a huge rock formation, about 100 kilometres wide, that is mostly under the ground. This rock formation includes Kata Tjuta (the Olgas) and Mount Connor.

Indigenous Australians have lived in the area for tens of thousands of years, and Uluru holds great cultural and spiritual significance for them. Climbing the rock goes against their wishes. In the past, people have been able to climb Uluru. There have been 37 deaths over the years. Although some deaths have been caused by falls (including a 16-year-old schoolboy in 1962), most have been the result of heart attacks.

UFO ACTIVITY AREA

UFO Capital of Australia?

Wycliffe Well is a tiny town along the Stuart Highway, on the edge of the Tanami Desert. Residents claim that it is the UFO capital of Australia and there have been more UFO sightings here than anywhere else in the country.

Why is it that UFO sightings always happen out in the middle of nowhere?

AUSTRALIA'S LONGEST DESERT ROAD

The Stuart Highway is Australia's longest road, running from Darwin in the Northern Territory to Port Augusta West in South Australia. It passes through the Tanami Desert, The Great Sandy Desert and the Great Victoria Desert, and is about 2710 kilometres long. Sections of the highway are used as emergency landing strips by the Royal Flying Doctor Service.

Are we there yet? Are we there yet? Are we there yet?

WATER IN THE DESERT

Kati Thanda–Lake Eyre in South Australia is the largest lake in the country, covering about 9500 kilometres. It's a salt lake and is in the desert. It is, however, dry most of the time. It is only completely filled up a few times each century during heavy rainfall. The river system that feeds the lake during these rains is called the Lake Eyre Basin. The basin covers areas of the Simpson Desert, the Sturts Stony Desert, the Strzelecki Desert and the Tirari Desert. When it is dry, the lakebed is covered in salt.

We went there. Walking on the salt is really weird. It's like being on an alien planet.

FUN DESERT FACTS

* A lot of Australia – 18 per cent – is classed as desert.

* Australia is the second-driest continent in the world, behind Antarctica, making it the driest inhabited continent in the world.

* The Atacama Desert in Chile and Peru is the world's driest desert. Parts of this desert have not seen rain in hundreds of years.

That's a long time to wait for a drink.

* Rainfall in Australian deserts is highly unpredictable and variable. It can sometimes cause flash flooding.

Ghost Town

On our trip, we stopped in Farina, which is on the edge of the Lake Eyre Basin. Farina is a deserted, desert town with crumbling buildings and hardly any tourists. It is a real-life, fair-dinkum GHOST TOWN. It is so cool. Visiting Farina was my idea. Mum and Dad were just going to drive past, but I'd read an adventure book about the RFDS that was set there and so I wanted to visit. The book is called *Remote Rescue* and is by Australian author George Ivanoff (see page 38 to find out how George was attacked by mosquitoes.).

There is so much interesting stuff in Australia's deserts, from salt lakes to ghost towns to that really BIG rock (and maybe UFOs?). Yep, it's dangerous. Yep, you could die if you're not careful. But . . . WOW! . . . Australian deserts are AMAZING!

Lake Eyre

CHAPTER 13

LEAFY DEATH

Who wants to go bush walking? Not me! Oh yeah, it's all fine and scenic and pretty . . . until you brush up against a stinging plant, or get bitten by a snake, or get hopelessly lost until you DIE of hunger, or you have no internet. I'll stick to walking on footpaths (to the video games shop).

AUSTRALIA'S TOP 3 DANGERS OF THE BUSH

1. Injury
2. Animals/insects
   (see Sections 1 and 2 for various chapters talking about everything that can kill you)
3. Plants

GETTING LOST

For thousands of years, Indigenous Australians lived in harmony with nature in the Australian bush. But ever since the arrival of white settlers, people have been getting lost . . . often dying as a result of being out in the harsh conditions.

In 1859, Constable Patrick Moylette was riding his horse from the Dandenong Police Station to the Britannia goldfields when he became lost in the bush. Although his horse eventually found its way back, Moylette was never seen again.

People have been getting lost and dying ever since.

In 1987, nine-year-old Patrick Hildebrand went ahead of his parents while walking along a track in Lilly Pilly Gully in Victoria's Wilsons Promontory. But he wandered off the path and was lost, never to be found.

Even today, people still often get lost in Australia's bushland. They are mostly bushwalkers and they are usually found within a few days. Although deaths are now rare, they still do occasionally happen.

INJURY

Injuring yourself is a real danger in the Australian bush, especially if you're alone. Many injured bushwalkers are rescued each year.

In October 2017, a woman fell while on a bushwalk in the Tidbinbilla Nature Reserve in the Australian Capital Territory, injuring her ankle. She was unable to walk. Luckily, there was mobile phone reception in the area and she called 000. Even so, search and rescue teams were not able to reach her until the following day, when she was winched to safety by helicopter.

ANIMALS/INSECTS

(See Sections 1 and 2 for a list of everything that can kill you!)

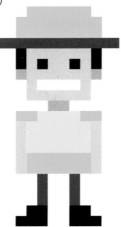

PLANTS

Plants You Should Not Eat:

- Black bean
- Strychnine tree
- Angel's trumpet
- Deadly nightshade
- Oleander

DO NOT eat any of these!

FACT BOX

Name
BLACK BEAN
Scientific name
Castanospermum australe
Other stuff you need to know
It has large pods filled with toxic seeds. If eaten they can cause vomiting and diarrhoea.

I never eat beans of any sort. Just. In. Case!

FACT BOX

Name
STRYCHNINE TREE
Scientific name
Strychnos nux-vomica
Other stuff you need to know
This tree has small, orange-coloured fruit that have poisonous seeds. If eaten in large amounts, the poison affects the nervous system, causing convulsions, paralysis and possibly death.

FACT BOX

Name

ANGEL'S TRUMPET

Scientific name

Brugmansia suaveolens

Other stuff you need to know

These plants have large red, white, orange or pink flowers. Although they are not native to Australia, they are now common. All parts of this plant are poisonous, particularly the leaves and seeds. If eaten it can cause diarrhoea, confusion, headaches, paralysis and possibly death.

FACT BOX

Name

DEADLY NIGHTSHADE

Scientific name

Atropa belladonna

Other stuff you need to know

Although it is not native to Australia, the tree is now common. The leaves and berries of this tree are poisonous. If eaten they can cause hysteria, hallucinations and possibly death. Eating a single leaf can be fatal. But you'd need to eat about 20 berries to die.

Well, the name is a bit of a giveaway, isn't it?

FACT BOX

Name

OLEANDER

Scientific name

Nerium oleander

Other stuff you need to know

Although they are not native to Australia, they are now common. This tree has white, red or pink flowers and is very poisonous. Eating any part of it can be fatal. Burning it is also dangerous, as the poison is carried in the smoke and fumes.

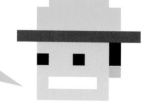

Plants You Should Not Touch:

- Milky mangrove
- Spurge
- Nettle
- Gympie gympie (giant stinging tree)
- Bindi

DO NOT touch any of these!

FACT BOX

Name
MILKY MANGROVE
Scientific name
Excoecaria agallocha
Other stuff you need to know
It is sometimes referred to as 'blind-your-eye-mangrove'. Its milky sap can cause skin irritation and blistering, and if it comes into contact with your eyes it can cause temporary blindness.

Um . . . why would anyone put the sap from a plant into their eyes?

FACT BOX

Name
SPURGE
Scientific name
Euphorbia
Other stuff you need to know
There are many species of spurge. The sap is called latex. It is sticky and hardens quickly, making it difficult to remove from skin. Contact with the sap can cause inflammation of the eyes, nose and mouth, as well as possible blindness.

FACT BOX

Name
NETTLE
Scientific name
Urticaceae
Other stuff you need to know
There are many nettle species, including herbs, shrubs, vines and small trees. Some of them have stinging hairs that can cause extreme pain if touched.

FACT BOX

Name
GYMPIE GYMPIE
Scientific name
Dendrocnide moroides
Other stuff you need to know
Also referred to as a 'giant stinging tree', it is actually a type of nettle. Stinging hairs on its stems, leaves and fruit can cause allergic reactions, swelling and severe pain.

FACT BOX

Name

BINDI

(or bindy)

Scientific name

Soliva sessilis and *Tribulus terrestris*

Other stuff you need to know

Both these plants are low-lying weeds. They are often found in the lawn areas of Australian gardens, causing a hazard to bare feet. Both plants have spiky burrs, but those of the *Tribulus terrestris* are larger and sharper.

One of my friends was always trying to get me to do the Bindi Run challenge. The challenge was to see who could make it from one end of her bindi-filled backyard to the other with bare feet. No way I was ever gonna do that!

BUSHWALKING SAFETY

WHEN OUT IN THE AUSTRALIAN BUSH:

DO:

✓ Make sure someone knows where you are going and when you will return.

✓ Take a mobile phone, matches, map and compass with you.

✓ Stick to paths and walking trails.

✓ Bring plenty of water with you.

✓ Bring food with you (even if it's just a snack).

> I never go anywhere without a chocolate bar.

DO NOT:

✗ If you are part of a group, DO NOT wander off on your own.

NOT QUITE SO DEAD · JUST DEAD · VERY DEAD · VERY VERY DEAD · NOT DEAD

Seriously, people . . . just don't put any unfamiliar plant in your mouth or rub it into your eyes.

SURVIVAL SKILLS IN THE AUSSIE BUSH

LIGHTING A FIRE

Being able to light a fire is important. As well as keeping you warm at night, the smoke could help rescuers find you. That's why you should always carry matches with you if you are bushwalking. If you don't have matches or a lighter, then you might have to light a fire the old-fashioned way . . . with friction.

You need to rub two pieces of wood together REALLY fast. And for a long time. It will make a small ember. Then you need to press some dry bark or paper against the ember to catch fire.

If you have the materials to create a bow drill, it will make things easier for you.

Bow drill

Yeah . . . I reckon it's just better to carry matches. This looks too hard.

FINDING FOOD

There is all sorts of 'bush tucker' to be found in the Australian bush. Indigenous Australians have known about it for thousands of year. (See Chapter 17)

FINDING WATER

DO NOT drink your own wee except as a last resort (see page 95). If you're lost in the bush, there are other ways to find water.

Water can collect on plants in the early morning and evening as dew. Press a piece of material (a handkerchief is ideal, but tear a piece off your shirt if you have nothing else) against grass and plant leaves to soak up the dew, then wring the water out into a container.

Condensation is another way to collect water. Tie a plastic bag over a tree branch with leaves and allow it to sit there for the day. The water released by the plant will condense on the inside of the bag.

So . . . basically this would mean you're drinking plant sweat.

Victorian Camper Survives Four Nights in the Bush

May 2018

Twenty-three year old camper, Sebastian Orefors, finally walked to safety after many hours lost in dense bushland in South Gippsland.

After slipping down a steep embankment while searching for a new campsite, Orefors became lost. When he didn't return, his mates at the original campsite raised the alarm and a search-and-rescue operation was mounted. Eighty-seven hours later, Orefors staggered onto a farming property, dehydrated and disorientated, but alive.

He survived by walking at night when it was coldest, in order to keep warm. When resting, he dug a hole and covered himself with dirt and ferns. He drank water from a creek at one point, but was otherwise without food or drink.

DON'T PANIC!

This is the most important thing. If you're lost, panicking can make the situation worse. It can result in bad decision-making and injury. It is important to stay calm, assess the situation, and make rational decisions.

Isn't that what's on the cover of *The Hitchhikers Guide to the Galaxy*?

I'm getting panicky just thinking about not panicking.

BUSHRANGERS

In the past, the Australian bush had an added danger – criminals! Bushrangers would rob and often kill travellers in the early days of Australian settlement. The most famous bushranger, Ned Kelly, has become an Australian icon.

Well, that's one thing I don't have to worry about.

Even though I begged them not to . . .

Even though I gave my parents all the info I collected about the DANGERS of the Australian bush . . . they still PUT MY LIFE AT RISK and made me go camping and bushwalking with them.

Remarkably, we SURVIVED!

And, I've gotta say that . . . well . . . I kind of enjoyed it. It was peaceful out there. And beautiful. We saw some amazing views. Sometimes, I guess, you just have to overcome your fears in order to experience cool stuff.

Not always! Just sometimes!

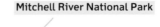

Mitchell River National Park

CHAPTER 14

DEATH FROM ABOVE

No matter where you go in Australia, there is one KILLER that you cannot get away from. At least, not unless you want to stay permanently indoors. And even *I* don't want to do that.

It's big! It's hot! And it's above us all. It's . . . [insert drumroll] . . . THE SUN!

The Sun

Our sun is actually a star, just like all those twinkling lights in the night sky. The difference is that our sun is a lot closer.

Earth orbits the sun, along with the other planets in our solar system. It's where we get our light and warmth, and without it, life on Earth could not exist.

The sun radiates three types of energy — infrared radiation (heat), visible light and ultraviolet light (also called UV light or UV radiation). Ultraviolet light can't be felt or seen so it's tricky to know when it's around. A little bit of ultraviolet light is fine. In fact, it's the best source of vitamin D. But too much can be damaging. It can give you sunburn and can lead to skin cancer.

Ultraviolet light also bounces off other surfaces, like snow, water and concrete, and it can go through clouds — which means you might get sunburnt on an overcast day.

SKIN CANCER

The biggest danger from being out in the sun, is the risk of skin cancer. Australia has one of the highest rates of skin cancer in the world. Two out of three Australians will get skin cancer by the time they are 70 years old. Over 100,000 cases are treated each year and over 2000 people in Australia die from skin cancer each year!

Skin cancer is a disease where skins cells are damaged and grow abnormally. Each time your cells are damaged by UV light from the sun, they become less able to repair themselves. And this increases your chances of getting skin cancer.

But it's not all doom and gloom. Skin cancer has one of the highest survival rates of all cancers and is very preventable with the right sun protection. You can protect yourself and reduce your chances of getting skin cancer. It's a matter of being sun smart!

> OMG! 2000! That's more people killed by this disease than by snakes and sharks and spiders and getting lost in the desert all put together!

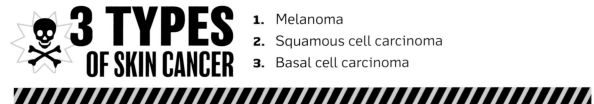

3 TYPES
OF SKIN CANCER

1. Melanoma
2. Squamous cell carcinoma
3. Basal cell carcinoma

FACT BOX

Name

MELANOMA

Appearance

It is usually flat with an uneven smudgy outline and can be brown, black, blue, red or grey. Nodular melanoma is a different, raised form of melanoma.

Other stuff you need to know

- Melanoma affects the melanocyte skin cells.
- This is the most dangerous skin cancer.
- It can grow very quickly.

FACT BOX

Name

SQUAMOUS CELL CARCINOMA

Appearance

It is usually a red, scaly spot.

Other stuff you need to know

- Squamous cell carcinoma affects the squamous skin cells.
- It grows slowly.
- It is not as dangerous as melanoma, but it can spread to other parts of the body.

FACT BOX

Name

BASAL CELL CARCINOMA

Appearance

It is usually a lump or dry, scaly area that is red, pale or pearly.

Other stuff you need to know

- Basal cell carcinoma affects the basal skin cells.
- It is the most common form of skin cancer.
- It is the least dangerous.
- It grows slowly.

Yikes! Always protect yourself in the sun!

Protect yourself from the sun with five easy steps . . .

Wear clothing to cover as much skin as possible

Apply SPF30 (or higher) broad-spectrum, water-resistant sunscreen

Wear a wide-brimmed hat

Stick to the shade as much as possible

Wear sunglasses

For more information on protecting yourself from skin cancer, check out the Cancer Council's SunSmart website: sunsmart.com.au

Go check it out straightaway. I mean . . . like . . . RIGHT NOW!

Holes in the Ozone Layer

The ozone layer is an invisible layer of gases in the Earth's atmosphere. It protects the Earth from getting too much harmful UV radiation from the sun.

Over the years, human beings have released pollutants into the atmosphere that have harmed and depleted the ozone layer. Although there has been an overall thinning, the worst areas are over Australia, the Arctic and Antarctica. Sometimes these thinner spots are referred to as holes in the ozone layer.

Since the discovery of the damage to the ozone layer, countries have banned the manufacture and use of harmful substances like the chlorofluorocarbons (CFC) that used to be in aerosol spray cans. The ozone layer is slowly repairing itself. Scientists expect the layer over Australia to get back to pre-1980 levels by 2050.

So it's more of an indentation than a hole.

UV LEVELS

The levels of UV are affected by time of day, time of year, cloud cover, altitude, how close you are to the equator and reflection. The World Health Organisation measures UV levels on a scale of 0 (low) to 11+ (extreme). When levels are 3 or higher, you should protect yourself. UV levels are reported in weather reports on the news, or on the Bureau of Meteorology website (bom.gov.au) and the SunSmart website (sunsmart.com.au). There's even a SunSmart app available. Don't wait for hot and sunny days to use sun protection. Remember UV!

My phone mostly has game apps. But now the SunSmart app is there too.

FACT BOX

All skin types can be damaged by too much UV. People with naturally very dark skin have a much lower risk of skin damage and skin cancer than people with a lighter skin tone, but everyone needs to take care out there! Especially kids. Children are more vulnerable to UV damage because their skin is more sensitive.

Pay attention, kiddies. Sunscreen! You don't want to be crispy-fried by the UV.

Checking

Most skin cancers can be treated successfully if discovered early. But without treatment, skin cancer can be DEADLY!

If you notice any difference to your skin – new moles, blotches or raised areas – get them checked out by your doctor. It could save your life!

If I had read all this stuff about the sun and UV and skin cancer a year ago, I think I would have said: 'That's it! I'm never going outside, ever again. I'll just stay in my room playing video games for EVER!'

But since being on this trip around Australia, seeing so many amazing things outdoors . . . well . . . I can't imagine staying inside all the time. Not even for the best video games. I actually want to go outside. And I WILL NOT let skin cancer STOP ME! I will protect myself with clothes, sunscreen, hat, sunnies and shade! I will go OUTSIDE and I will stay SAFE. So there!

CHAPTER 15

SANDY DROWNING DEATH

In the previous chapter I covered the dangers of the sun. Surely that's enough to keep you away from the beach? No? Well, remember the sharks? And the jellyfish? And the octopuses? Still want more? Okay then . . . how's this . . .

DROWNING!

But going down to the beach on a hot summer's day is such an Aussie thing to do. So if you do go to the beach . . .

Be sensible!

Be careful!

And don't DROWN!

WARNING: DANGER OF DROWNING

Australia has a lot of desert areas, but it also has a lot of coastline. And given how popular going to the beach is in Australia, drowning is a real danger. According to Royal Life Saving Australia, 50 people drowned on Australian beaches from July 2016 to June 2017, with the number of people injured or needing rescue in the hundreds. But many of these deaths and injuries can be avoided with a little common sense.

TOP 2 WATER HAZARDS AT THE BEACH

1. Rip currents
2. Waves

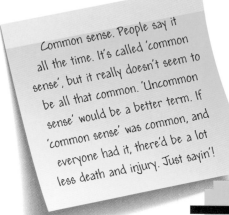

Common sense. People say it all the time. It's called 'common sense', but it really doesn't seem to be all that common. 'Uncommon sense' would be a better term. If 'common sense' was common, and everyone had it, there'd be a lot less death and injury. Just sayin'!

RIP CURRENTS

At the beach, water is pushed onto the shore in waves. After the waves breaks, the water needs to find a way back into the ocean. A rip current, known as a 'rip', is the path that water takes back to the sea. Rips will usually appear as dark channels between the white, breaking waves heading for the shore. They will often form in deeper areas of water, like between two sandbanks. Sometimes a rip can be mild, at other times quite strong. Some beaches are known for their strong, permanent rip currents.

Rips are dangerous because most people don't realise they're there and are caught by surprise. They can suddenly find themselves swept out into deep water. People panic and fight against the current, eventually becoming exhausted, and are carried away. This can be dangerous even for a strong swimmer.

Even the name is ominous. Rip currents. Rips. I just keep imagining people being ripped apart!

MYTH

Many people think that a rip can pull you under the water. This is not true! A rip current cannot pull you under the water.

WAVES

The larger the waves, the greater the danger of being knocked over. But sometimes, large waves can hit unexpectedly.

Surging waves are those that never really break on the shore. Instead, they surge forward a long way up onto the sand. This type of unexpected wave can knock a person off their feet. Non-swimmers, elderly people and young children might find themselves knocked over and then swept off into deep water. Children should always be supervised at the beach and remain within arm's length of an adult if in the water.

Dumping waves curl over and crash down with great strength. They often happen around shallow sandbanks. While a person is not likely to drown by getting hit by a dumping wave, they can be injured. People have suffered broken limbs, head injuries and even spinal injuries when hit unexpectedly by one of these strong waves.

Wave to the waves. LOL.

RIP SURVIVAL

WHAT TO DO IF CAUGHT IN A RIP

DO NOT:

✕ DO NOT try to swim straight back to shore. Fighting against the current like this is difficult and could exhaust you.

✕ DO NOT panic. When you panic, you can make bad decisions.

DO:

✓ STAY CALM! Your body is able to naturally float and the current will not pull you under the water. Float with the current until it releases you.

✓ Or . . . swim parallel to the shore, towards the waves. This will take you out of the rip current and towards shallower water. The waves can then help you to get back to shore.

✓ Raise your arms and wave them to attract attention if you need help.

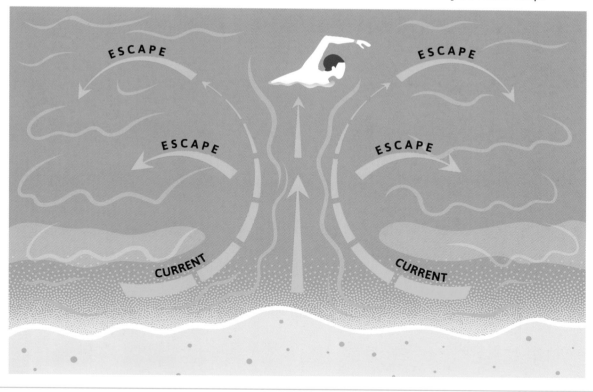

Wolverine Rip Rescue

26 March 2016

Actor and *X-Men* star Hugh Jackman saved his own son from a rip current at Sydney's Bondi Beach.

After a world tour to promote his new film, *Eddie the Eagle*, Jackman returned to Australia to spend a day on the beach with his family. But as the water grew rougher a sudden rip current caught his son, Oscar, off guard, pulling him into deeper water. Jackman rescued his son from the rip, bringing him up onto a sandbank.

Surf lifesavers were on hand to rescue others as the rip current grew worse. Jackman stayed to help out. But after multiple rescues, the conditions grew more dangerous and the swimming flags were moved to another part of the beach.

Wow! Rescued by Wolverine. How cool is that!

SURVIVAL TIPS

DO NOT:

✗ Beaches known for rip currents and other dangers are signposted. DO NOT swim there.

✗ DO NOT turn your back on the water while standing in rough conditions on a beach.

DO:

✓ On patrolled beaches, DO swim between the flags that mark the safe area.

✓ DO keep an eye out for rip currents and avoid them.

✓ DO follow any instructions from lifeguards and surf lifesavers.

Two-coloured red and yellow flags are used to mark patrolled areas of the beach where it is safe to swim. Single-coloured yellow flags indicate potential danger, warning swimmers to be extra careful. Single-coloured red flags mean that the beach is closed to swimmers. Single-coloured blue flags indicate areas for surfing and board riding. Two-coloured red and white flags are used for emergency evacuations.

FACT BOX

Name

RED WARATAH ANEMONE

Scientific name

Actinia tenebrosa

Size

About 4 centimetres wide

Prey

Plankton and small fish

Habitat

Rocky shores

Location

Southern coasts from Shark Bay in Western Australia, to Heron Island in Queensland

Other stuff you need to know

- Red waratah anemone have bright red tentacles which they use to sting and capture their prey.
- They creep along rocks towards their prey.
- Young red waratah anemone emerge from the adult's mouth, fully formed.

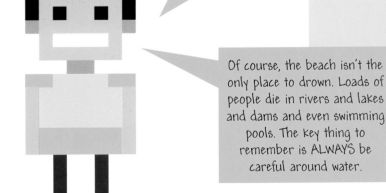

Now that is a WEIRD way to be born! Sounds like something from a horror film.

Of course, the beach isn't the only place to drown. Loads of people die in rivers and lakes and dams and even swimming pools. The key thing to remember is ALWAYS be careful around water.

I know lots of people like the beach. And I guess I kind of do as well . . . mostly to go looking in rock pools (my fave rock pool find was a red waratah anemone). There are so many interesting creatures and shells and things you can find in rock pools. BUT . . . you don't want to be enjoying a nice day at the beach and then end up DEAD!!!! So, you know, be careful.

CHAPTER 16

THE FOUR ELEMENTS OF DEATH

It doesn't matter where you are in Australia – in the bush, in the desert, in a city – sudden, unexpected DEATH can strike at any moment. The four elements of air, water, fire and earth can be the bringers of DESTRUCTION. Say hello to the four types of natural disaster that could KILL YOU.

THE FOUR ELEMENTS OF DEATH

AIR
Cyclones

WATER
Floods

FIRE
Bushfires

EARTH
Earthquakes

AIR: CYCLONES

Cyclones are large spiralling storms that form over tropical seas where warm air rises. They gather strength as they travel over water towards land. Cyclones bring heavy rains and winds that can sometimes be strong enough to uproot trees and destroy buildings. Once a cyclone passes over land it begins to weaken.

Every cyclone has an eye – a calm, central area that varies from 10 to 100 kilometres wide. The eye can have light winds and a blue sky, but is surrounded by a dense wall of clouds with the fast winds.

Some of Australia's worst natural disasters have been cyclones. Cyclones happen every year along the northern coasts of Western Australia, the Northern Territory and Queensland. An average of ten will develop over Australian waters each year, with about six of them reaching land.

While all cyclones have strong winds and are potentially dangerous, not all of them will cause death and destruction. There is a ranking system that puts cyclones in categories from 1 to 5.

CYCLONE CATEGORIES

CATEGORY 1
Minor
90-124 km/h wind gusts.
Minor damage to crops and trees.

CATEGORY 5
Extreme
Over 280 km/h wind gusts.
Extreme, widespread destruction.

CATEGORY 2
Moderate
125-164 km/h wind gusts.
Minor damage to buildings.
Moderate damage to trees.
Heavier damage to some crops
and other plants.

CATEGORY 4
Major
225-279 km/h wind gusts.
Major damage to buildings.
Dangerous airborne debris.

CATEGORY 3
Strong
165-224 km/h wind gusts.
Moderate damage to buildings.
Heavier damage to trees and
other plants.

I reckon it's pretty weird how they give cyclones people's names, like Tracy and Billy. There's a list of approved names that is put together by a special committee at the World Meteorological Organisation. Seriously! I reckon cyclones need more unusual names. Names to make them stand out a bit. Like Caractacus . . . or Murgatroyd.

They all sound pretty dangerous to me. I think I'll go hide in a cellar.

AUSTRALIA'S TOP 5 DEADLIEST CYCLONES

1. Cyclone Mahina
2. Cyclone Tracy
3. Cyclone Innisfail
4. Cyclone Mackay
5. Cyclone Ada

FACT BOX

Name
CYCLONE MAHINA

Landfall
Bathurst Bay, Queensland

Year
1899

Strength
Category 5

Lives lost
Over 400 (deadliest natural disaster in Australian history)

FACT BOX

Name
CYCLONE TRACY

Landfall
Darwin, Northern Territory

Year
1974

Strength
Category 4

Lives lost
More than 65 dead, thousands injured, more than 32,000 people evacuated

FACT BOX

Name
CYCLONE INNISFAIL

Landfall
Innisfail, Queensland

Year
1974

Strength
Category 4

Lives lost
More than 60

FACT BOX

Name
CYCLONE MACKAY

Landfall
Mackay, Queensland

Year
1918

Strength
Category 4

Lives lost
30

FACT BOX

Name

CYCLONE ADA

Landfall

Whitsundays, Queensland

Year

1970

Strength

Category 4

Lives lost

14

No one seems to agree on exactly how many people died in some of the cyclones. Different articles list different death tolls.

WATER: FLOODS

Even though Australia is dry and full of desert areas, it still suffers from floods. In fact, floods are Australia's costliest natural disasters. Damage estimates can run into the billions of dollars. But there is also a high death toll, with most deaths occurring when people attempt to cross floodwaters.

There are different types of floods. Most floods are caused by unusually high rainfall, which can cause rivers to overflow. Sometimes there are flash floods when drains and creeks can't cope with the extra water. Seawater floods occur when storms push massive waves up onto a coast, flooding low-lying areas. Occasionally, floods are caused by bursting dams, which can happen in an earthquake.

AUSTRALIA'S TOP 3 DEADLIEST FLOODS

1. Gundagai
2. Clermont
3. Melbourne

FACT BOX

Location

GUNDAGAI, NEW SOUTH WALES

Year

1952

Caused by

The Murrumbidgee River overflowing

Lives lost

89

FACT BOX

Location
CLERMONT, QUEENSLAND
Year
1916
Caused by
Runoff from creeks and catchments areas due to heavy rainfall from a cyclone
Lives lost
65

FACT BOX

Location
MELBOURNE, VICTORIA
Year
1934
Caused by
Unusually high rainfall
Lives lost
36

FIRE: BUSHFIRES

Australia is a hot and dry country, so bushfires are a constant danger. In dry weather, plants in the bush dry out, so a single spark can ignite a fire. Strong hot winds can fan a bushfire, making it spread rapidly, and can blow embers across long distances to start more fires. Bushfires have been caused by lightning strikes, sparks from machinery, fallen powerlines and campfires that have not been extinguished properly. Sometimes they have even been started deliberately. TOTAL FIRE BANS are often declared on hot, dry, windy days in an attempt to reduce the risk for bushfire.

But bushfires are also part of Australia's natural lifecycle. Certain trees, like the mountain ash, need fire for their seeds to germinate. Other eucalyptus trees have below-ground shoots (lignotubers), which are encouraged to grow by fire. And there are many plants in the Australian bush whose seed germination is helped by the smoke in a bushfire. For thousands of years, Australia's Indigenous people used to deliberately burn areas of bush, facilitating this cycle.

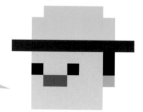

So these are like the plant equivalent of a phoenix — the mythical bird that is born from its own ashes.

AUSTRALIA'S TOP 5 DEADLIEST BUSHFIRES

1. Black Saturday
2. Ash Wednesday
3. Black Friday
4. Black Tuesday
5. Gippsland Fires

FACT BOX

Name
BLACK SATURDAY

Location
Victoria

Year
2009

Lives lost
173

2009! That's not all that long ago. Mum and Dad actually remember watching this on the news.

FACT BOX

Name
ASH WEDNESDAY

Location
Victoria and South Australia

Year
1983

Lives lost
75

FACT BOX

Name
BLACK FRIDAY

Location
Victoria

Year
1939

Lives lost
71

FACT BOX

Name
BLACK TUESDAY

Location
Tasmania

Year
1967

Lives lost
62

FACT BOX

Name
GIPPSLAND FIRES

Location
Victoria

Year
1926

Lives lost
60

NOT DEAD · NOT QUITE SO DEAD · JUST DEAD · VERY DEAD · VERY VERY DEAD

EXPLODING TREES

Eucalyptus oil catches fire very easily. And eucalyptus trees are full of eucalyptus oil. They burn fast. There have even been reports of these trees exploding during bush fires. Whether or not this really happens is a debated topic, with many claiming it to be a myth.

EARTH: EARTHQUAKES

The Earth is made up of large sections, called tectonic plates. It is the movement of these plates that causes earthquakes. These earthquakes are a sudden shaking of the ground. Many earthquakes only cause a mild disturbance and no damage. But some can be violent, causing buildings to collapse and the ground to split. Australia is not a high-risk area for earthquakes, but even so, it has suffered the effects of some large and devastating ones.

Earthquakes are categorised according to their magnitude (how strong they are at their source), with the Richter scale of 1 to 10.

RICHTER SCALE	TYPE	WHAT CAN HAPPEN
1.0–1.9	Micro	Not felt.
2.0–2.9	Minor	Recorded by instruments but not actually felt by people.
3.0–3.9	Minor	Can sometimes be felt. No damage.
4.0–4.9	Light	Noticeable shaking. Can be minor damage.
5.0–5.9	Moderate	Can cause reasonable damage to poorly constructed buildings.
6.0–6.9	Strong	Moderate to major damage. Only slight damage to earthquake resistant buildings.
7.0–7.9	Major	Damage to most buildings.
8.0–8.9	Great	Serious damage to most buildings.
9.0–10.0	Extreme	Extreme damage.

AUSTRALIA'S TOP 3 DEADLIEST EARTHQUAKES

1. Newcastle
2. Beachport
3. Meckering

FACT BOX

Location
NEWCASTLE, NEW SOUTH WALES

Year
1989

Magnitude
5.4

Financial damage
$4 billion

Lives lost
13 people dead; more than 160 injured

FACT BOX

Location
BEACHPORT, SOUTH AUSTRALIA

Year
1897

Magnitude
6.5

Lives lost
No deaths, 50 injured

FACT BOX

Location
MECKERING, WESTERN AUSTRALIA

Year
1968

Magnitude
6.5

Financial damage
$18 million

Lives lost
No deaths, over 20 injured

The earthquake at Meckering in 1968 caused the railway line to buckle and the highway to split.

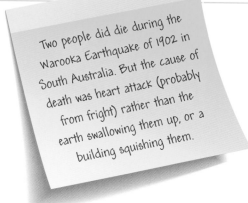

Two people did die during the Warooka Earthquake of 1902 in South Australia. But the cause of death was heart attack (probably from fright) rather than the earth swallowing them up, or a building squishing them.

Can hail be a disaster? Not usually. But sometimes hailstones can get pretty BIG! Australia's biggest hailstones were recorded in Sydney in 1999. They were about the size of cricket balls. No one died. (Yay!) But the hailstorm caused over $1.7 billion damage. (Boo!)

While Australia has had some really bad natural disasters, they don't really happen all that often. So perhaps, living in fear of them is a bit silly.

CHAPTER 17

NOT DEATH (BUSH TUCKER AND BUSH MEDICINE)

Okay, okay . . . so this chapter's a bit different. It's all been death and destruction so far (and I promise there's more to come), but I really wanted to document bush tucker and bush medicine. A lot of places around Australia, like Uluru and Kata Tjuta (also known as the Olgas) and Lake Mungo, have tours conducted by Indigenous guides. And the guides often talk about how their ancestors lived off the land. I reckon that's really interesting. And knowing about this stuff could help you survive if you got lost in the bush or the desert.

Bush Tucker

Kangaroos, wallabies, emus, bush turkeys, goannas, snakes and insects are just some of the native animals that are known to Indigenous Australians as bush tucker. And there are a wide variety of native plants as well, including fruits, nuts, roots, tubers and bulbs. While this sort of food was strange and unfamiliar to European settlers when they first arrived in Australia, many of these delicacies have since made their way into the mainstream of Australia's culinary landscape. Many restaurants will serve emu and kangaroo. You can buy riberry jam or cooking oil flavoured with lemon myrtle. The flavours of the Australian bush are many and varied and absolutely delicious.

AUSTRALIA'S TOP 2 MOST AMAZING BUSH TUCKER FOODS According to me.

1. Witchetty grubs
2. Honey ants

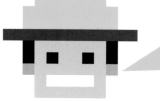

A kangaroo and an emu are the two main animals on Australia's coat of arms. And both are edible.

Name

WITCHETTY GRUB – THE LARVAL STAGE OF COSSID WOOD MOTHS

Scientific name

Endoxyla leucomochla

How to eat them

They can be eaten raw (and live) or lightly roasted in hot ash. If having them live, it's best to eat them tail first so they don't bite you. They are nutritious and high in protein.

OMG! Food that bites back! Ahhhhhhhh!

Other stuff you need to know

● Witchetty grubs are probably the most famous type of bush tucker. They feed on the root sap of the witchetty bush (*Acacia kempeana*). They are harvested by digging up the roots of these bushes.

● Other grubs can also be eaten and are also usually referred to as witchetty grubs, even though, technically, they are not. These fat, white, wood-boring grubs include the larval stage of other wood moths, swift moths and longicorn beetles.

FACT FILE

Name

HONEY ANT

(a general term covering several species)

Scientific name

Species in the *Camponotus* and *Melophorus* groupings.

How to eat them

Raw. You don't actually eat the entire ant, just the bloated, honey-filled abdomen.

Other stuff you need to know

● Aphids and scale insects eat the sap of plants and then secrete a sticky, sugary liquid from their anus. It's called honeydew. Honey ants then eat the honeydew. But they don't just eat up all the honeydew they can find. They have a system to store up their food when there's plenty of it. The worker ants collect the honeydew and bring it home to their nest, where it is stored by special ants called repletes. The repletes eat the honeydew and store it in their abdomens, which become bloated and stretched. They then feed other ants by regurgitating the honeydew into their mouths.

● A full sac of honeydew is about the size of a blueberry.

Boy, I'm glad I'm not a honey ant.

● Finding honey ants is a real skill. Yellow honey ants make their nests at the base of mulga trees, while dark honey ants make their nests at the base of turkey bushes. The repletes spend their lives underground in galleries, deep within the ant nests.

So basically, you'd be eating an ant's stomach stuffed full of aphid poo. Yum, yum!

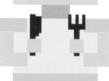

Decisions. Decisions!

AUSTRALIA'S ~~TOP~~ *Random* 4 BUSH TUCKER PLANTS

1. Lilly pilly
2. Quandong
3. Bunya Pine
4. Desert yam

There are so many edible plants that are native to Australia. Too many to include here. So I just randomly picked four.

FACT BOX

Common name

LILLY PILLY

Scientific name

Syzygium

Other stuff you need to know

- A wide variety of lilly pilly plants exist, with berries that are pink, white or purple.

- Most will have a large inedible seed in the centre. But the berries of the small-leaved lilly pilly (*Syzygium luehmannii*), called riberries, have smaller edible seeds. They also have a stronger flavour.

FACT BOX

Common name

QUANDONG

Scientific name

Santalum acuminatum

Other stuff you need to know

- Quandongs grow in desert areas with spinifex grass and mulga bushes.

- The fruit are apple-sized and bright red. They are high in protein compared to most other fruit. There is a stone in the centre of the fruit, and the kernel within the stone of certain varieties is edible. But the kernel of some varieties may be poisonous.

Hmmm . . . maybe I just won't eat any kernels.

FACT BOX

Common name

BUNYA PINE

Scientific name

Araucaria bidwillii

Other stuff you need to know

- Bunya pines are large trees that can grow up to 80 metres high.

- They grow in the mountains of south-eastern Queensland and northern New South Wales.

- They produce pine cones full of nuts, which can be eaten raw or cooked.

FACT BOX

Common name

DESERT YAM

Scientific name

Ipomoea costata

Other stuff you need to know

- The top part of the plant is a running vine, with the tubers deep under the ground. The tubers are 12–20 centimetres long and 5–18 centimetres wide, and each plant can have up to 20 of them.

- Desert yams are traditionally cooked under coals.

Bush Medicine

Indigenous Australians have long used native flora and fauna to treat sickness and injury. Some, such as tea tree oil and eucalyptus oil, have come to be used in products you can buy on the supermarket shelves, such as tea tree oil acne cream and eucalyptus throat lozenges. There are other, more obscure, remedies that are not widely used.

AUSTRALIA'S ~~TOP~~ Random 4 BUSH MEDICINE

1. The leaves of the pepperberry plant (*Tasmannia lanceolata*) can be pounded and soaked in water to make an antiseptic liquid for sores and wounds.

2. Common plate fungus (*Phellinus rimosus*) can be dried and burned, the smoke inhaled to relieve headaches, coughs and nasal congestion.

3. Emu berry (*Grewia retusifolia*) roots can be roasted in ashes, then pounded and soaked in water. The liquid is then used to bath sore eyes.

4. A paste made from crushed witchetty grubs can be used to soothe burns.

I'd rather crush a witchetty grub than eat it.

CONCLUSION

So . . . I'm beginning to think that even though Australia is DANGEROUS . . . maybe the good things outweigh the bad? Apart from the occasional natural disaster, staying alive seems to be a matter of common sense. It's about avoiding the dangerous things . . . which is not really all that hard (especially when they are signposted). Maybe I should try to relax a bit.

SECTION FOUR

EVERYTHING ELSE

(NOT ALL OF IT INVOLVING DEATH)

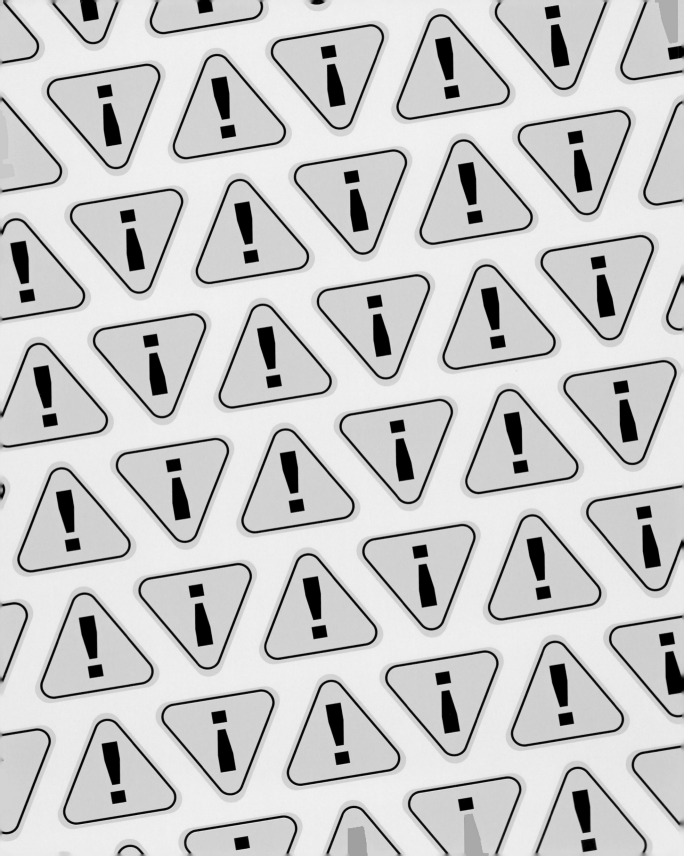

CHAPTER 18

CIVILISATION

So . . . this is the hard bit. I've collected all this info about how DEADLY and DANGEROUS Australia is – about how the animals and the environment are OUT TO GET YOU – when, in fact, the most dangerous and deadly things in this country are actually people. Yep! Us!

Before the European settlement of Australia, the Indigenous peoples lived in harmony with the land. They lived this way for THOUSANDS of years. Then European settlers came and kinda messed things up. They took the land from the Indigenous people, and even killed off a lot of them. Slowly, over time, animals have been driven into extinction, introduced species have caused havoc with the ecosystem and pollution has destroyed the environment. They even exploded nuclear bombs in the desert.

> Yep! The biggest threat is . . . US!

Invasion

For the people who first came to Australia from England, it was settlement. For the Indigenous people already living here, it was invasion. Their land was taken from them. Many of them were murdered. And a sad history of mistreatment began. It is only in relatively recent times, that the Australian Government put measures into place to try to make amends. Custodianship of many sites sacred to the Indigenous people have been returned to them. And on 13 February 2008, Prime Minister Kevin Rudd made a formal apology to Australia's Indigenous peoples.

> My mum and dad remember this happening. They reckon it was a really important thing. I watched the vid on YouTube. It's just one little word, but it's amazing how important the word 'sorry' can be.

EXTINCTION

Australia is home to more animal species than any other developed country; and most of this wildlife is unique to Australia – including:

- 87 per cent of mammal species
- 93 per cent of reptile species
- 94 per cent of frog species
- 45 per cent of bird species.

Since European settlement, many animals, have become extinct. Hunting, introduced species and destruction of the environment have had a devastating effect.

The thylacine (Tasmanian tiger) is perhaps Australia's most famous extinct animal, but the Tasmanian emu, desert rat-kangaroo, pig-footed bandicoot and the dusky flying fox are just some of the other animals that have disappeared.

Australia is at risk of losing even more of its animals, including keystone animals. While the loss of any species is a tragedy, the loss of a keystone species is dangerous to the ecosystem.

WHAT IS A KEYSTONE ANIMAL?

A keystone animal may be a predator, like the dingo – its existence keeps down the numbers of pests such as foxes and feral cats. But a keystone animal can also help the ecosystem in other ways. For example over 200 plants depend upon the southern cassowary for the spread of its seeds.

> Wow! This is amazing! It shows how connected nature is. It's like a game of Jenga. Pull out the wrong bit and everything falls over.

FACT FILE

Name

THYLACINE

Also known as
Tasmanian tiger, Tasmanian wolf

Scientific name
Thylacinus cynocephalus

Prey
Bandicoots, possums and other marsupials, small rodents, birds

Other stuff you need to know

- Thylacines were large carnivorous marsupials.
- Although extinct on the mainland prior to European settlement, thylacines thrived on the island of Tasmania.

- They were hunted into extinction by settlers who considered them a danger to their sheep and poultry.
- The last-known thylacine, named Benjamin, died on 7 September 1936 at the Beaumaris Zoo in Hobart.
- Because of unconfirmed sightings, it is believed that thylacines may have survived in the wild beyond 1936, but they were officially declared extinct in the 1980s.

> That's heartbreaking! It died alone . . . the last of its kind.

NOT QUITE SO DEAD · JUST DEAD · VERY DEAD · NOT DEAD · VERY **VERY** DEAD

AUSTRALIA'S ~~TOP~~ *Random* 5 ENDANGERED ~~KEYSTONE~~ ANIMALS

(there are too many to list them all)

1. Southern cassowary
2. Grey-headed flying fox
3. Gilbert's potoroo
4. Grey nurse shark
5. Tasmanian devil

This makes me so sad.

WHAT'S BEING DONE ABOUT IT?

But it's not all DOOM and GLOOM . . .

The Australian Government has put together the Threatened Species Strategy, which works at protecting endangered species, improving habitats and creating safe havens. There are also numerous conservation organisations dedicated to educating people and minimising threats to animals and relocating animals in danger.

Invasive Species

European settlers brought many plants and animals into Australia. Some of these have proven to be damaging to the ecosystem.

AUSTRALIA'S TOP 11 INVASIVE ANIMAL SPECIES

1. Cane toad
2. European rabbit
3. Red fox
4. European honey bee
5. Brumbies (feral horses)
6. Feral camels
7. Feral cats
8. Deer
9. Feral goats
10. Feral pigs
11. Water buffalo

Brumby herds cause extensive damage TO VEGETATION, RESULTING IN EROSION.

The European rabbit was introduced into Australia in 1857 for recreational hunting and food.

Feral goats have been responsible for spreading introduced weeds across the country through seeds in their dung.

It is estimated that 3 per cent of Australians are allergic to honey bee stings.

Australia has the largest population of feral camels in the world.

There are now six species of deer found in Australia – fallow, red, hog, rusa, chital, and sambar.

Because of **wetland destruction caused by water buffalo,** the populations of crocodiles, turtles and waterbirds have decreased.

Red foxes

The red fox was introduced into Australia in 1855 for recreational hunting.

Pigs were brought to Sydney as livestock in 1788, but by the 1880s they had run wild over large parts of Australia.

Feral cats

have become a danger to native species such as bilbies, bandicoots and numbats.

FACT FILE

Name
CANE TOAD

Also known as
Giant neotropical toad, marine toad

Scientific name
Bufo marinus (or *Rhinella marinus*)

Poison
Cane toads have poison glands on their shoulders. If ingested, the poison causes rapid heartbeat, excessive salivation, hallucination, convulsions and paralysis.

But only if you eat or lick it. Eww! As if you would!

Other stuff you need to know
Cane toads were introduced in 1935 from South America. They were introduced to try to control the cane beetle (which is an Australian native) that was destroying sugar cane crops. But cane toads breed rapidly, have no predators in Australia and are poisonous to many Australian animals. They are now in plague numbers and are considered an extreme danger to the ecosystem.

CANE TOAD PRODUCTS

There are so many cane toads in Australia that they are now being used to make leather goods, including handbags, wallets and purses. You can even buy stuffed cane toads.

Oh yeah! I'd really like a stuffed toad on my bedside table . . . NOT!

INVASIVE PLANT SPECIES

While imported animals get all the publicity, there are also many introduced plants that are a danger. Weeds are the greatest problem. So while the poisonous deadly nightshade plant might sound more dramatic, the rubber vine, which smothers other trees and shrubs, causes much more damage.

AUSTRALIA'S TOP 7 INVASIVE WEEDS
(according to the Australian National Botanic Gardens)

1. Rubber vine (*Cryptostegia grandiflora*)
2. Blue thunbergia (*Thunbergia grandiflora*)
3. Hymenachne (*Hymenachne amplexicaulis*)
4. Aleman grass (*Echinochloa polystachia*)
5. Para grass (*Brachiaria mutica*)
6. Giant sensitive plant (*Mimosa pigra*)
7. Athel pine (*Tamarix aphylla*)

I'm having flashbacks to an old *Doctor Who* episode where plants came to life and attacked people. And the cause of all the mayhem? An invasive introduced species . . . introduced from Outer Space!

The Environment

Civilisation has a habit of destroying the environment — from air pollution caused by the exhaust from cars, to the destruction of native habitats. We burn coal instead of using renewable sources of energy such a solar power. We put so much rubbish into landfill and, even worse, throw much of it onto the ground and into waterways.

NUCLEAR WEAPONS

For many years, Australia allowed the United Kingdom to test its nuclear weapons on Australian shores. It began on 3 October 1952 when a nuclear device was exploded on the Montebello Islands off the coast of Western Australia. The first mainland test occurred on 15 October 1953 at Emu Field in the Great Victoria Desert, South Australia. A second device was exploded two weeks later. A further seven tests occurred at Maralinga between 1956 and 1963.

WHAT CAN YOU DO ABOUT IT?

Single-use plastic bags have been banned in most of Australia, with the remaining two states soon to follow. Renewable sources of energy, such as solar power and wind power, are being used more often. Recycling is becoming more widespread. And even individuals are doing their bit by composting food scraps rather than throwing them in the bin.

OMG! This is just UNBELIEVABLE! We allowed NUCLEAR BOMBS to be EXPLODED in Australia. Really? Who does that?

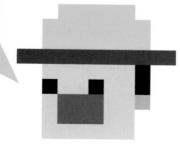

Okay, now that I've done the hard bit, I can do the fun stuff. I've found out Australia is not all DEATH and DESTRUCTION. And civilisation isn't all BAD. It is possible to travel through this country and have FUN!

Blue thunbergia

CHAPTER 19

BIG THINGS

Australia is a BIG country! It has large deserts. It has an enormous rock formation that includes Uluru and Kata Tjuta. It also has really BIG mountains, like Mount Kosciuszko in New South Wales and Mount Ossa in Tasmania.

But that's not enough, is it? Having BIG natural wonders is just the tip of the iceberg (although we don't have any of those). We also build big things. Really, REALLY BIG things!

FACT BOX

BIGGEST CATTLE STATION IN THE WORLD

Name

ANNA CREEK STATION

Location

160 kilometres east of Coober Pedy, South Australia.

Size

15,746 kilometres^2

Other stuff you need to know

It is bigger than some countries, including Lebanon, Malta and Nauru.

I wonder if Anna Creek Station could declare independence and become a country?

TOP 2 LONGEST FENCES IN THE WORLD

1. Dingo Fence
2. State Barrier Fence of Western Australia

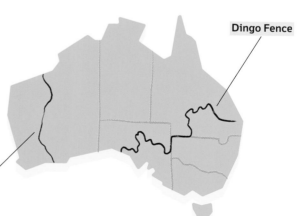

Dingo Fence

State Barrier Fence of Western Australia

FACT BOX

Name

DINGO FENCE

Location

From Jimbour in Queensland to Fowlers Bay in South Australia

Length

5614 kilometres

Other stuff you need to know

It was built in the 1880s to protect sheep in the south-eastern parts of Australia from dingoes. It holds the Guinness World Record for longest fence.

> Wow! That's the same distance as Melbourne to Sydney and back . . . over three times!

> Both these fences used to be longer but they got shortened.

FACT BOX

Name

STATE BARRIER FENCE OF WESTERN AUSTRALIA

Also known as

Rabbit-Proof Fence

Location

Western Australia

Length

1170 kilometres

Other stuff you need to know

It is a pest-exclusion fence built between 1901 and 1907. It is actually three connecting fences.

GIANT ROADSIDE ATTRACTIONS

Australia has a heap of GIANT tourist attractions. Major roadways are dotted with REALLY BIG fruit, vegetables and animals, designed to make people stop and take a look . . . and maybe spend some money. The first of these was the 13 metre-long concrete banana along the Pacific Highway at Coffs Harbour, which was constructed in 1964. It was supposed to attract drivers to the nearby banana stall. It is now part of The Big Banana Fun Park and is claimed to be the biggest banana in the world.

BIGGEST GIANT FRUIT

The big pineapple in Woombye on the Sunshine Coast in Queensland. Built in 1971, it is 16 metres high and 6 metres wide.

> Australia is obsessed with these BIG THINGS. We've got fruit, vegetables, fish, animals, people and even objects all over the country. It's really WEIRD!

BIGGEST GIANT ANIMAL

The biggest animal is the giant Gippsland earthworm on the Bass Highway in Bass, Gippsland, Victoria. Although it is only 4 metres high, it is an impressive 250 metres long. It used to house a museum dedicated to the local giant Gippsland earthworm.

Which leads me to this.

FACT BOX

Name

GIANT GIPPSLAND EARTHWORM

Scientific name

Megascolides australis

Size

Average length of 1 metre, but can grow up to 3 metres in length

Location

Bass River Valley, in South Gippsland

OMG! A worm as long as my bedroom!!!!!

Other stuff you need to know

- The giant Gippsland earthworm is one of the largest earthworms in the world.

- When first discovered in the 1870s, the people who found it thought it was a snake.

Imagine trying to shear that!

GIANT ANIMAL WITH THE COOLEST NAME

'Rambo', the Big Merino in Goulburn, New South Wales. Built in 1985, it is 15 metres x 18 metres.

That **is** a pretty cool name for a giant sheep.

WEIRDEST GIANT THINGS

- Big bench in Broken Hill, New South Wales. Built in 2002, it is 2.5 times bigger than a standard park bench.

- The big golden guitar on the New England Highway in Tamworth, New South Wales. Built in 1988 it is 12 metres x 4 metres. It's a giant replica of the trophies given out at Tamworth Country Music Festival.

- The big boxing crocodile on the Arnhem Highway at the town of Humpty Doo in the Northern Territory. Built in 1988, it is 13 metres high. It was modelled on Australia's logo for the 1983 America's Cup Yacht Race.

- The Big Easel, in Morton Park, Queensland. Built in 1999, it is 25 metres tall and holds a 7 metres × 10 metres reproduction of one of Van Gogh's Sunflower paintings.

> What? Why?

> But I'm gonna finish with one more REALLY BIG wonder of nature . . .

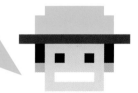

FUN FACT

* The Sydney Opera House is pretty big. Finished in 1973, over one million tiles were used on its famous curved roof.

> So, the Sydney Opera House isn't really dangerous. Not unless you try to do something stupid . . . like climb its roof and fall off.

FACT BOX

THE WORLD'S BIGGEST CORAL REEF

Name

THE GREAT BARRIER REEF

Location
Off the north-eastern coast of Queensland

Length
Over 2300 kilometres

Other stuff you need to know
The reef is home to over 16,000 species of fish and 3000 species of molluscs.

> Been there! It is AMAZING!

THE DEAD-O-METER RATING FOR AUSTRALIA'S BIG THINGS IS ...

NOT DEAD!

CHAPTER 20

RANDOM STUFF

So . . . I found out lots of interesting stuff about Australia whilst researching how to stay alive. Not all of it is LIFE THREATENING. Some of it is GROUNDBREAKING. Some of it is FUNNY. Some of it is STUPID! Survival isn't just about avoiding what can MUTILATE, MAIM and KILL you . . . it's also about knowledge. So, here's some random knowledge for you . . .

Slang

Some people might say that Australians have MURDERED the English language. Certainly, Australians have adapted the language with a variety of colourful slang words, curious sayings and weird diminutives (words that have been shortened). Australian slang is itself known by the slang term 'strine'.

G'day, mate!

TOP 10
AUSSIE DIMINUTIVES

1. Australian → Aussie
2. Good day → G'day
3. Afternoon → Arvo
4. Mosquito → Mozzie
5. Tradesperson → Tradie
6. Cup of tea or coffee → Cuppa
7. Service station → Servo
8. Aggravated → Aggro
9. Barbecue → Barbie
10. Chewing gum → Chewie

TOP 11
AUSSIE SLANG WORDS

1. Youse
   plural of you

2. Reckon
   to have an opinion

3. Spewin'
   not happy

   > This is my favourite!

4. Strewth
   exclamation of disbelief or shock

5. Anklebiter
   child

6. Barrack
   support

7. Bludger
   lazy person

   > You mean it's not a Quidditch ball?

8. Dunny
   toilet

9. Drongo
   idiot

10. Shonky
    something not to be relied upon

11. Bonza
    excellent

> Strewth! I reckon this is a bonza list! See what I did there?

TOP 10
WEIRDEST AUSSIE SLANG PHRASES

1. She'll be apples
   everything will be okay

2. Happy as Larry
   very happy

3. Spitting the dummy
   getting upset

4. Like a stunned mullet
   dazed

5. Put the moz on
   have a bad influence

6. Mad as a cut snake
   very angry

7. Going off like a frog in a sock
   very, very excited

8. Don't come the raw prawn with me
   don't treat me like an idiot

9. Better than a poke in the eye with a blunt stick
   better than nothing

10. Carrying on like a pork chop
    behaving silly

> I've never even heard of some of these!

THE DEAD-O-METER RATING FOR STRINE IS ...

CACTUS!
VERY VERY DEAD

> Aussie slang for dead.

BELT UP

Australia is dangerous and deadly in a lot of ways . . . but it has attempted to keep people safe on the roads for a long time. It was the first country to make the wearing of seatbelts compulsory. Victoria passed the world's first seatbelt law in 1970, making it compulsory for drivers and front-seat passengers to wear seatbelts.

> So . . . in a car crash the people up front would survive while those in back would be thrown from their seats to their DEATHS! Hmm . . . does anyone else see a problem here?

Vegemite

It's dark brown and sticky. It comes in a jar and you spread it on toast. It looks disgusting but tastes delicious. While people outside Australia might think it's a bit strange, most Aussies reckon Vegemite is pretty good.

Vegemite was launched on the market in 1923. It's made from brewers' yeast extract (a by-product of making beer), along with salt, malt extract from barley, vegetable extract and B vitamins. But the exact recipe is a closely guarded secret.

> Mmmm . . . doesn't that sound appetising?

AUSSIE INVENTIONS

Lots of amazing and weird things have been invented in Australia, including . . .

- The Hills Hoist – a height-adjustable, rotating clothes line
- The esky – a portable cooling box for food and drink
- Black box flight recorder – a device that records the instrument readings and the voices in the cockpit of a plane, it is capable of surviving a crash and helps with crash investigations
- Polymer bank notes – plastic money
- Cochlear implant – bionic ear
- Wi-fi technology
- The splayd – combination of spoon, knife and fork
- Duel-flush toilet
- Permanent-crease clothing

I don't think the splayd caught on.

Hills Hoist

AUSTRALIA'S EARLIEST INVENTIONS

- The didgeridoo – A musical wind instrument made from a hollow wooden tube.
- The boomerang – weapon made of wood. When thrown correctly, it will return to the thrower.

Personal Random Observation: Australia has this weird thing of turning murdering criminals into celebrities. It all started with Ned Kelly. He was a bushranger. He robbed people. He killed people. But after his execution he became an icon. There are statues of him. There are books and films about him. And he's on loads of souvenirs. He's treated more like a hero than a criminal.

LET ME OUT OF HERE . . .

Back in 1933, Western Australia tried to secede from the Commonwealth of Australia and become its own country. The state government held a referendum, in which two thirds of Western Australians actually voted to secede, and put together an official request. The federal government said NO.

SPACE LITTER

In 1979, the abandoned space station *Skylab* fell out of orbit and mostly disintegrated in Earth's atmosphere. But small pieces of debris made it through the atmosphere, scattering over the Nullarbor and the Western Australian town of Esperance. When NASA officials visited the town to examine the debris, they were presented with a $400 littering fine. NASA never paid it!

I wonder if the fine was meant to be a joke?

CONCLUSION

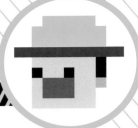

Australia is a weird and wonderful place, isn't it? Sometimes deadly and dangerous. Sometimes glorious and wondrous. But ALWAYS amazing!

We, as a civilsation, have done so much here ... both good and bad. I guess that's just how the human race works. We do incredibly creative things, like inventing new technology, adapting language and building giant statues of fruit. And Vegemite! Don't forget the Vegemite. But we also do great harm to our environment. We pollute. We hunt animals into extinction. We are careless with the planet which we call home. If only we could all just take a step back and appreciate where we live.

I think everyone should take a trip around whatever country they live in, to get an appreciation of how awesome it is. Australia is an amazing place. But so is every other place on Earth. Each and every other place, from the driest desert to the densest jungle. Every place has its uniqueness. Every place has something incredible to offer the world. We need to appreciate it. Because if we appreciated it, we might not wreck it.

I'm gonna make a promise to myself right now – that I will always try to appreciate where I live. This country, Australia! This world that it's a part of, the planet Earth.

THE BIT AT THE END

I'M ALIVE!

I didn't DIE!

I'm pretty happy about that.

Not only did I survive my parents dragging me around Australia . . . but . . . well, I did actually kinda enjoy it. But shhhh! Don't tell them. I don't want them to think that they were right.

Although, I guess they were. Sure, there were scary bits. There was some stuff I didn't enjoy (like the really loooooong drives along really loooooong desert roads). But there were also lots of AMAZING things.

The scenery!

The animals!

The people!

My fave things . . .

- Taking a helicopter flight around Uluru. Breathtaking!

- Snorkelling the Great Barrier Reef

- Getting to cuddle a koala

- Eating a barbecued witchetty grub (Don't knock it until you've tried it)

- Spending time with my parents (Don't tell them that either)

I guess I've learned some stuff along the way. Like, you can't let fear stop you from doing things. I was scared of all the things in Australia that could harm me. I didn't want to travel around the country. But I faced that fear. I did travel. And it was BRILLIANT!

So, yeah . . . Australia is DANGEROUS! And there are things that could KILL YOU! But mostly, it's a matter of being sensible. Don't go swimming where there are warning signs about crocs or sharks. Don't go trying to pat random snakes or spiders. Don't go wandering off in the desert alone without food or water or sunscreen. If you're sensible, you can avoid the DANGER and enjoy the GOOD STUFF.

And there is so much GOOD STUFF!

So, if you ever get the chance, go experience this amazing country. If your parents ever say, 'How about a holiday around Australia?', don't let fear stop you from saying, 'Sure thing!'

Now that it's all over,
I can say . . .
Surviving Australia . . .
It was a piece of cake!

Lamington

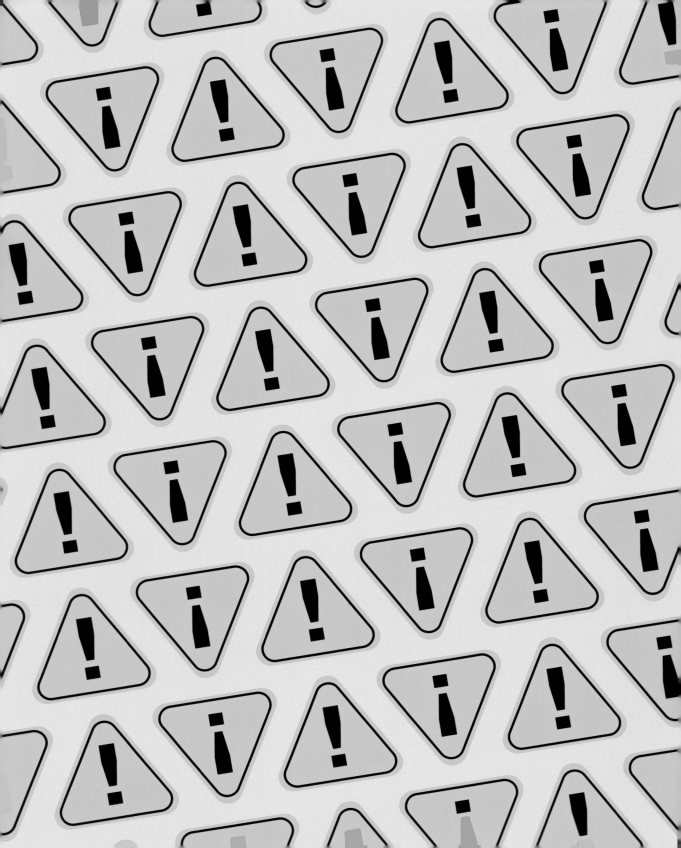

GLOSSARY

These are some words and terms used in the guide that you might not know. So here's a chance to expand your knowledge.

allergic reaction
This is when a person reacts badly to a substance. The substance might be eaten or breathed in or injected by a bite or sting. Some allergic reactions are minor and might only cause itching or sneezing; but others can result in life-threatening anaphylactic shock.

Alzheimer's disease
A brain disease that gets worse over time. It affects mainly older people and causes memory loss and confusion.

anaphylactic shock
Allergic reactions to bites and stings can lead to anaphylactic shock. Anaphylactic shock causes blood pressure to drop, making people feel weak and dizzy, and their airways will close up, making it hard to breath. People can die from this.

arachnophobia
A phobia where a person has an irrational fear of spiders.

arid
Dry, lacking moisture.

billabong
A waterhole.

bow drill
A tool that uses friction to start a fire.

brain haemorrhage
An exploding artery in the brain that causes bleeding, which kills brain cells.

bush tucker
Food found in the bush using Indigenous methods.

cardiac arrest
This means your heart stops beating.

cardiovascular disease
This means a person has problems with their heart and/or blood vessels.

citronella
A type of citrus-scented grass originating from Southern Asia. Oil from this grass can be used as an insect repellent.

cold-blooded
Some animals are cold-blooded and this means that the temperature of their bodies is effected and changed by the environment around them.

CPR
CPR stands for cardiopulmonary resuscitation. It involves chest compressions (pressing down on the chest over the heart) to make the heart beat, and rescue breaths (breathing into the victim's mouth) to get air into their lungs.

dehydration/dehydrated
When water is lost or taken out of something.

ecosystem
The environment surrounding a community of living things.

flash flooding
A sudden deluge of water caused by heavy and sudden rain.

germinate
When a plant seed begins to grow and put out shoots.

hallucinations
A hallucination is when you hear and/or see things that aren't really there.

heart failure
That's when your heart can't pump enough blood around your body.

meteorology
The study of the weather and its patterns.

natural disaster
A natural event that causes great destruction and often loss of life. For example, floods, bushfires and droughts.

necrotising bite
This means the bite will cause a large chunk of your flesh to die and rot away.

Ned Kelly
He was a bushranger and leader of the Kelly Gang. He is famous for wearing a suit of armour in a standoff against the police at Glenrowan in 1880.

paralysis
A state in which a person can't move and has lost control of the muscles in their body.

poison/poinsonous
A poisonous substance is toxic if ingested or touched.

prehistoric
The time period in history before a record was kept of events and happenings.

pressure immobilisation bandage
This is a bandage that wraps an entire limb tightly and also has a splint to stop it from moving.

Richter scale
A man named Charles Richter, who lived in America in the last century, invented a system of measurement used to gauge the strength of earthquakes.

rip current
A fast current that can cause swimmers to be pulled further from shore and out to sea.

sap
The liquid of a tree or plant.

Or the Aussie slang for a weak person

secede
To withdraw from an organisation or government.

species
A classification for plants, animals or organisms that have similar qualities.

tourniquet
A bandage or cord tied tightly around a limb to slow or stop the flow of blood.

toxic
Something that is capable of causing illness or death.

UV
UV stands for ultraviolet, particularly ultraviolet light from the sun.

venom
A substance which is toxic if injected through a bite or sting.

zooids
An organic creature that can move and live separately from the larger organism it usually lives with.

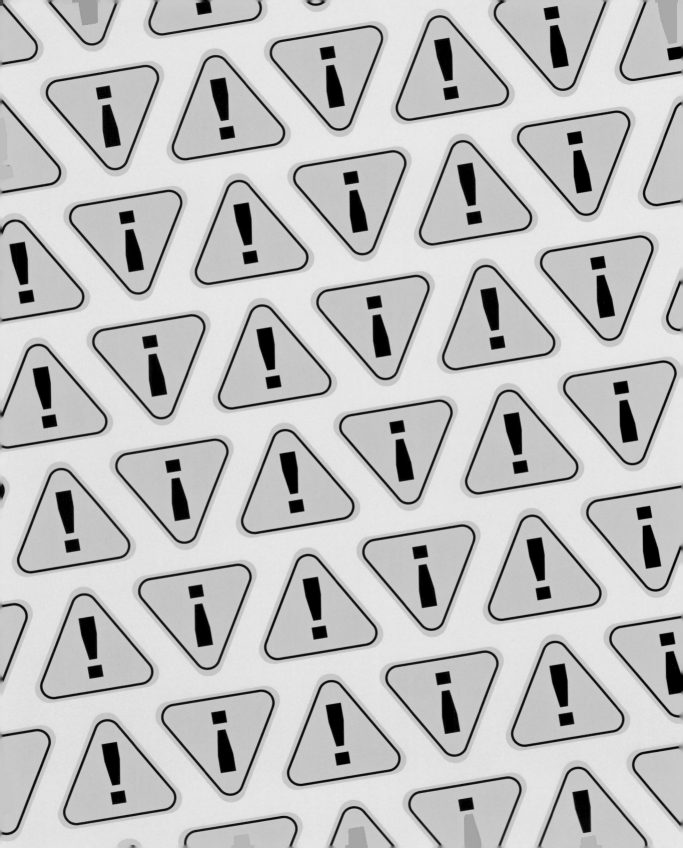

FURTHER READING

Want to know more about Australia? There are lots of great books and websites out there. Here are some of the main references I used when researching this guide.

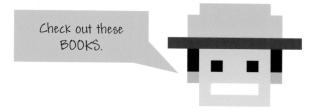

Check out these BOOKS.

Edgar, Graham J. (2000) *Australian Marine Life: the plants and animals of temperate waters*, revised edition. Australia: New Holland Publishers.

This is a great reference book about everything that lives in Australia's seas.

Egerton, Louise (Ed) (2005) *Encyclopedia of Australian Wildlife*, revised edition. Sydney: Reader's Digest Australia.

Birds, reptiles, mammals . . . they're all in here.

Holland, Elizabeth, et al (2009) *Bush Tucker and Medicine of the Ngaanyatjarra Lands*. Melbourne: Pearson Australia.

This book focuses on particular groups of Indigenous peoples, mostly from Western Australia. It is a good introduction to the ideas of bush tucker and bush medicine.

Mirtschin, Peter; Rasmussen, Arne R. & Weinstein, Scott A. (2017) *Australia's Dangerous Snakes: Identification, Biology and Envenoming*. Victoria: CSIRO Publishing.

This is a guide to all the snakes that could kill or harm you. Fun reading!

Whyte, Robert & Anderson, Greg (2017) *A Field Guide to Spiders of Australia*. Victoria: CSIRO Publishing.

This book covers all of Australia's spiders . . . not just the dangerous ones.

Various authors (2010) *Disasters in Australia* (4-book series). Melbourne: Pearson Australia.

These four books give a basic introduction to bushfires, cyclones, earthquakes and floods in Australia.

Check out these WEBSITES.

Australian Geographic
australiangeographic.com.au

This is a great site with LOTS of articles about Australia's plants, animals and environment.

Australian Shark Attack File
taronga.org.au/conservation-and-science/australian-shark-attack-file

This site has everything you need to know about shark attacks, but also has general information about sharks.

Bureau of Meteorology
www.bom.gov.au

This site is about more than just looking up what the weather it going to be like (although you can do that). There's heaps of information here about weather conditions, climate change and the environment.

CrocBITE: Worldwide Crocodilian Attack Database
www.crocodile-attack.info

This site has everything you need to know about crocodile attacks in Australia and all over the world, but also has general information about crocs.

Sunsmart
www.sunsmart.com.au

Run by the Cancer Council Victoria, this site has loads of info about the dangers of the sun and how to protect yourself.

About the Author

George Ivanoff is a Melbourne author who's written more than 100 books for kids and teens, including the interactive You Choose series, the RFDS Adventures and the OTHER WORLDS series. His books have been shortlisted for numerous awards, and he's even managed to win a few of them, including a YABBA for *You Choose: The Treasure of Dead Man's Cove*.

George has travelled extensively around Australia, visiting all sorts of places, from Lake Mungo to Lake Eyre, from Alice Springs to Adelaide, from the desolate Oodnadatta Track (where he got three flat tyres) to the isolated ghost town of Farina (where he didn't see any ghosts). He's had a scenic helicopter flight around Uluru and been taken on a tour of remote schools in Western Australia's Pilbara region on a light aeroplane. He has cuddled a koala, fed a kangaroo, patted a dingo and held a thorny devil in the palm of his hand (it was very thorny).

In 2015 he and his family embarked on a two and a half week road trip from Melbourne to Uluru and back. Along with three other families, they travelled convoy-style through the outback, camping along the way and experiencing the country up close. George thinks Australia is a pretty amazing place and intends to see a lot more of it in coming years.

His Aussie expeditions have come in handy for his writing. The choice of settings for the RFDS Adventures were based on his travels. His trip to Lake Mungo inspired his geography school reader, *Lost at Lake Mungo*. And now, there's this book!

George drinks too much coffee, eats too much chocolate and watches too much *Doctor Who*. He has one wife, two children and an uncontrollable imagination.

ACKNOWLEDGEMENTS

No book is ever the product of just the author. There are always other people who help and contribute – from supportive family and friends to beta readers, editors and proofreaders. Every book is the result of the efforts of many people working together. So, here's a shout-out to the people who've helped me with this book.

My family have never been anything less than 100% supportive. My kids put up with me constantly saying things like 'I can't just now, I've got a chapter to finish' and 'we can go to the movies after I've met this deadline'. As well as simply putting up with me (which is no mean feat), my wife Kerri was a sounding board for ideas right from the start, as well as my beta reader . . . and always, my inspiration.

My publisher Holly was instrumental in guiding this project, from initial suggestions, to working out the direction and enthusiastically supporting the idea of having a fictional character narrating this nonfiction guide.

They say that a good editor is worth their weight in gold. Well, I'd up that to platinum for my editor, Mary. Her eye for detail, her patience and her inexhaustible enthusiasm have resulted in a book that is way better than anything I could have done on my own. And not only was she editing, she was also fact checking – which is a heck of a BIG task for this sort of book. Her being a *Doctor Who* fan was the icing on the cake!

I'm not sure what I was expecting in terms of book design,

but what I got, completely blew me away. Designer Astred has done an extraordinary job of giving this book a standout, unique look. It's about as far away as you can get from an educational book . . . which is perfect! Because although this book probably is educational, mostly, it's meant to be FUN! And Astred has captured that sense of fun.

So to all these people, my sincere thanks! I literally could not have done it without you.

I should also acknowledge the debt I owe to all those books and websites (a select number of which are listed under Further Reading) that I consulted during the researching of this guide. Thank you to all those authors and compilers of facts. While I have done my best to cross-reference information and find the best sources, mistakes do sometimes slip through. If there are any errors contained within these pages, they are entirely my fault. And I apologise in advance.

BTW . . . Does anyone ever read the acknowledgements page? Or is this just filler? Well, if there is anyone still reading this . . . thanks . . . but it's over now . . . you can go. Bye!

IMAGE AND ILLUSTRATION CREDITS